HIDE & SEEK

500
CAMPARI

HIDE & SEEK | MELBOURNE 2

CONTENTS

004 / HIT THE STREETS

026 / TREASURE TROVE

Let's face it: too much choice can can leave you stuck like a deer in the decision-making headlights. New cafes pop up faster in Melbourne than trends started on Twitter, and it seems there isn't a laneway left in its rubbish-tip peace, as buildings surrounding these graffiti alleys are constantly claimed for shops, bars and whatnot. Don't get me wrong – I still love Melbourne for all of its personality – but my head constantly spins with all of the options for where to eat, drink, shop and hang out.

Hide & Seek Melbourne 2 can be your way out of this First World headache. We've pulled together 40 *more* interesting and unique places, both in the city centre and inner suburbs, which we believe are a cut above the rest. The book is divided into four, colour-coded chapters: **HIT THE STREETS** (places to see or activities that prove Melbourne, even with its sheen of cool galleries, is still a fun and friendly city); **TREASURE TROVE** (shopping experiences that will make you happy to spend a few bucks on something special); **FEELING PECKISH?** (eateries that preserve Melbourne's reputation as a foodie's paradise, but without the increasingly hefty prices); and **NIGHT OWL** (places where you can get a drink, maybe have a late-night eat or a dance, or even play a few computer games). There's something for everyone here, no matter what your tastes or interests, and in all cases, we've got you covered when it comes to your hard-earned dollars.

I'd like to take this opportunity to say thank you to the freelancers whose enthusiasm and dedication have made ***Hide & Seek Melbourne 2*** possible: to Erika Budiman for her incredible design and photography skills, to Michelle Bennett for her amazing editorial efforts, to Megan Ellis for her typesetting genius and to our in-house cartographer Emily Maffei for her funky maps.

Our stellar team of writers are in-the-know Melburnians, who love everything about this graffiti-splashed city. If you find somewhere hidden in Melbourne that you think others should seek out, send your email to **info@hideseek.com.au**. Otherwise, the blank page at the back of the book gives you space to record your own Melbourne discoveries.

Cheers,

Melissa Krafchek | Series editor

ABOUT THE WRITERS

VANESSA MURRAY
Vanessa is a freelance writer who lives and works in Melbourne. She enjoys its bikes and cafes and hidey-holes, its arty-crafty vibe and its people-watching potential. Find her at www.vanessa-murray.com or @MsVanessaMurray.

SAMANTHA WILSON
When she's not cuddling her cat Spartan, Sam lives the life of a freelance writer and rock'n'roll tragic. Like a large portion of the Melbourne population, she's a transplanted 'Perthie', and loves her adopted hometown for its cool bands, fab shopping and endless pubs. She's yet to master dressing appropriately for the fickle Melbourne climate, though.

CHAD PARKHILL
Chad is a Melbourne-based culture vulture, caffeine addict, music critic, and freelance writer and editor. His interests include cocktail culture, critical theory, the history of sexuality, and subjecting others to his suspect taste in music (aka 'DJing').

DALE CAMPISI
Dale has co-written a bunch of guidebooks including *Go Explore Melbourne* (Explore Australia) and *Eating and Drinking Melbourne* (Hardie Grant). Although he now lives half his life across Bass Strait in Hobart, and is the current editor of Tasmanian culture quarterly *Island*, he still spends an inordinate amount of time exploring, eating and drinking on the streets of Melbourne.

JANA RAUS

Jana has a deep love for Melbourne, and one of her favourite things is exploring the city on her motorbike, street by street, cafe by cafe, bar by bar. She currently works as a publisher, and has penned reviews on bars, restaurants, films screened at the Melbourne International Film Festival and theatrical performances at the Melbourne Arts Festival. There are still many more Melburnian roads left for her to cover.

RYAN SMITH

Ryan was born in Adelaide and made the obvious choice to move to Melbourne as soon as he possibly could. On any given day, you can find him playing with fabric swatches, trawling through thrift stores and flea markets for hidden treasures, reorganising his (or someone else's) apartment interior, or drinking Japanese beer at a corner table while feverishly filling notebooks with his scrawl.

MICHAEL BRADY

Michael is a Melbourne artist and 'gallerist', as well as being a co-writer of *Go Explore Melbourne* (Explore Australia) and *Eating and Drinking Melbourne* (Hardie Grant). He doesn't drive a car, so he walks a lot (which is a great way of getting to know the city). He enjoys observing the Bourke Street Mall from his balcony while dreaming of living in a gallery one day soon.

REBECCA L. STEWART

Rebecca likes travelling through places with names like Burkina Faso and Kyrgyzstan, but is usually found in her home office in glamorous Footscray. As a seasoned Melbourne bar reviewer, Rebecca has developed an aversion to astroturf, deliberately exposed pipes and wires, the idea that VB is 'retro', paying $14 for tapas and places where trackies are unwelcome. Find her work at: http://boostew.com

HIT THE STREETS

12

TRAM SESSIONS

LEAVE YOUR IPOD AT HOME

Consider this the perfect marriage between two of Melbourne's most loved and well-known things: its bustling music scene and trams. Born out of a group of friends' love of both (OK, so they're more into the music), Tram Sessions is like the best surprise party you've ever been to – except everyone gets a surprise, not just the birthday boy or girl.

The concept is simple but brilliant. A completely unannounced band boards a tram, sets up its gear and spends some time entertaining the passengers. It's like a more intimate and purposeful version of a flash mob*. Everyone wins: the bands get exposure and the passengers are treated to delightful, unexpected, free entertainment. Commuters struggling on their way home after a stressful day are cheered up, and those who are at first embarrassed, staring out the window trying to ignore the shenanigans, more often than not end up joining in the fun.

One of the best things is how the Tram Sessions crew matches the various routes with different types of music. So, for example, the City Circle's old-fashioned trams are perfect for some mellow jazz or other tunes that use an old-school upright bass, while the number 96 from Brunswick to St Kilda will likely have something more upbeat.

Now you could just cruise Melbourne's trams hoping to catch a secret gig, but here's a clue: these public-transport parties happen on Zone 1 Yarra Trams. Better yet, follow Tram Sessions on Twitter or Facebook, but try to keep it hush-hush, OK? We don't want to spoil the surprise for the other passengers.

> HIT THE STREETS

Various (tram-line) locations
www.tramsessions.com
Anywhere, any time!

'ENCYCLO' TRIVIA

* A flash mob is a large group of people who come together via text messages or social media. The group meets in a public space then briefly performs an out-there, though seemingly pointless, act – to the bemusement of onlookers – before dispersing as quickly as it formed.

MISS
FOX

MISS FOX

GET YOUR GLAMOUR ON

Much like the Marie Antoinette of beauty parlours, Miss Fox is dedicated to glamour over grunge and opulence over restraint. Looking and feeling fabulous is the name of the game here; eating cake is an optional extra*.

Smack-bang in the heart of the CBD (where many of its clients work), this self-declared quintessential beauty, spa and wellness destination provides a blissful escape from day-to-day reality. Whether you're sipping fine bubbly from a crystal flute while having your nails minxed*, or soaking in a heavenly milk bath, a visit to Miss Fox is your ticket to forget your worries and simply *indulge*.

So, what'll it be? Miss Fox's treatment menu is as extensive as a French queen's wig collection, spanning the spectrum of cosmetic and therapeutic procedures (including some you've probably never heard of). It's a tough choice. You may think you want your eyebrows shaped and your hair curled, until you notice the tantalising range of spa facials available. Booked in for a body polish or massage? Better allow time for a make-up session just in case. Staff are cherry-picked for their expertise and charm, and products used are top-shelf and free of chemical nasties.

Admittedly, this kind of champagne lifestyle doesn't always come on a beer budget. But there are plenty of affordable treatments, and it costs nothing to enjoy the sumptuous surroundings. For Miss Fox is a sight to behold! Plush couches and shiny lacquered floorboards, stylish light fittings and soaring ceilings – it's a vintage-luxe sensation. Pink flamingos and cheeky pin-up prints add a touch of fun to the mix.

Glamour and good times: now there's a foxy combination …

> HIT THE STREETS

Levels 1–3, 285 Little Collins St, Melbourne
1300 647 736
www.missfox.com.au
Open Tues–Fri 11am–7pm, Sat 10am–5pm (advance bookings strongly recommended)

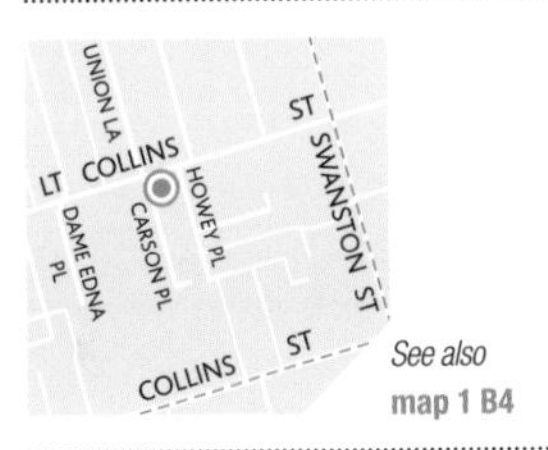

See also **map 1 B4**

'ENCYCLO' TRIVIA

* 'Let them eat cake.' While this famous phrase is attributed to the notorious M-A, it also applies to Miss Fox, where gourmet sweeties are served on request.

* Popular with celebs like Lady Gaga, minxing involves the application of hand-cut, adhesive nail designs. It's ultra blingy and exclusive to Miss Fox in Melbourne.

> HIT THE STREETS

THE POWER OF CREATIVITY

If there's one thing that cities are generally short of, it's space. So to come across a place like Newport's Substation feels like a luxury indeed. This not-for-profit, community-based arts centre has space in spades – and we all know that you need space to truly create.

Built in the hollowed-out shell of a former massive electrical substation – hence the name – this vast place is perfect for a multitude of artistic and cultural expressions. The blank-canvas nature of the space and the solidity of the historic, industrial building mean that it can be adapted for almost any purpose, and the Substation takes full advantage of this. A major part of this complex is its gallery, where six exhibition spaces showcase monthly changing work from emerging and established contemporary artists. Artworks range from photography to sculpture, painting to new media, installation art to interactive displays.

Then there's the humungous Performance Hall, with its lofty ceiling, vast wooden floor and dramatic red drapes framing stunning, floor-to-ceiling arched windows. Here you can catch a range of events, from dance and music to comedy and theatre performances. This is also the hub for community happenings, where things like Red Cross blood-donation drives occur, and the place for an artists' market, where you can pick up some fabulous handmade jewellery, clothing, artworks and the like on the first Saturday of the month.

If you'd rather do some creating of your own, there are regular workshops and classes held here too, so you can brush up on your watercolour painting or try something new, like Serbian folk dance. Check the website for the latest goings-on, and then get ready to embrace this space.

> HIT THE STREETS

1 Market St, Newport
(03) 9391 1110
www.thesubstation.org.au
Gallery open Thurs–Sun 11am–5pm; Artists' market open first Sat of every month (except Jan) 10am–4pm; check the website for event and class times

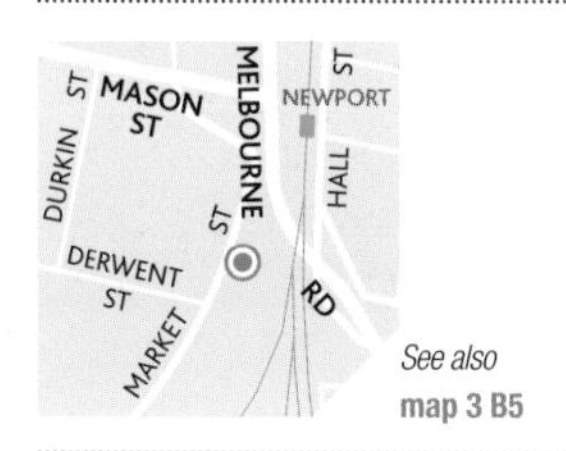

See also **map 3 B5**

LOSE YOUR INTERGALACTIC VIRGINITY

Dear Sir Richard Branson,
We understand your need for perspective on humanity's insignificance – your desire to break the bounds of gravity and take a giant step into the universe. Virgin Galactic? A commendably modern and adventurous endeavour. But Sir Richard, please, there is really no need to leave our humble planet to get your space fix.

We cordially invite you to visit the fair city of Melbourne and to take a stroll along the St Kilda foreshore, where a model of the solar system awaits. You read correctly: the sun, all eight planets and an asteroid are presented here, at a scale of one to one billion, for your viewing pleasure. Even more impressively, Port Phillip's fetching crescent curve is perfectly shaped for this very journey, as the pint-sized sun can be viewed from every one of the mini-me planets.

Your journey will begin at Marine Pier, where a blazing metallic ball 139 cm in diameter (that's the sun, FYI) awaits. You'll continue along the shared bike and pedestrian path to Mercury, then to Venus, to Earth and Earth's moon, then on past Mars, Jupiter, Saturn, Uranus and Neptune at a giddy pace. Finally, right down past Princes Pier, 5.9 km from the sun, you'll reach that dastardly asteroid, Pluto, just 0.24 cm in diameter.

Think of the billions, even zillions of dollars you'll save. Not to mention the workout you'll get, when you consider that every centimetre you walk is equivalent to 10 000 galactic kilometres. So what do you say, Sir Richard? Impressed? You're welcome. Drinks are on you.

Love,
Hide & Seek

> HIT THE STREETS

From Marine Pier, St Kilda Beach,
to the Boulevard, Port Melbourne
www.melbournesolarsystem.com.au
Open 24/7

See **map 4**

MAILBOX 141

POSTMODERN POSTMAN PAT

Once upon a time, way back in the 20th century, there lived a row of wooden mailboxes in an office building foyer. Back then, the mailboxes' job was to keep letters safe and sound until they were collected by their owners. Flash forward to the 21st century and these humble letterboxes have been transformed into Mailbox 141, a mini gallery showcasing the teeniest artworks in town. Trust Melbourne to come up with yet another way to display art in an unexpected, out-of-the-way spot!

Mailbox 141 blurs the line between public art space and gallery as we know it: climb the foyer stairs and you'll see what we mean. Each cute little mailbox has a back-lit glass window for viewing the work of emerging creatives, each with a knack for making things 'reet petite'. Exhibitions change monthly and range from printmaking to illustration to photography and even to sculpture. Anything goes as long as it's fresh, experimental and fits the bill … er, make that box. You need to get in real close for a good look here, so bow down and bring out your inner peeping Tom before Postman Pat catches you in the act.

This public art space shares a building with Tessuti Fabrics, so just look out for Tessuti's button-and-needle sign (with the number 141 on it) and you'll be signed, sealed and delivered to one of this city's most unique exhibition spaces.

> HIT THE STREETS

141 Flinders La, Melbourne
www.mailbox-141.artabase.net
Open Mon–Fri 8am–6pm, Sat 10am–5pm

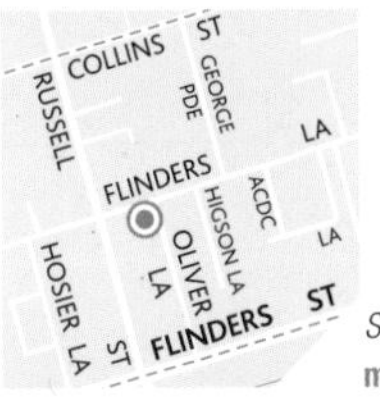

See also **map 1 C4**

SUN THEATRE

A BEACON IN THE WEST

There's more than one sun in Yarraville. Aside from the regular one, there's an iconic, red-and-yellow neon sun that sits atop the historic Sun Theatre. This Sun has been entertaining the masses for decades – with ups and downs along the way – and currently screens the latest new movie releases in the classy surrounds of a restored Art Deco* theatre.

The original Sun opened in 1938 in all her glory. Back then the theatre contained just one cinema, but it was large enough to seat 1050 patrons and screenings were sold out most Saturday nights. To attract mothers to the theatre, a separate 'pram room' was built. Babies were assigned a number, and when they cried their number would flash on the screen to alert their mothers! The arrival of television saw the buzzing crowds sadly dwindle, and, after a period as a Greek cinema, the Sun was eventually closed by the Health Department due to unsanitary carpets – ew!

After years of neglect, it was reduced to little more than a derelict, hollow box. The current owners purchased it in 1995 and set to work restoring it to its former beauty – except this time it would entertain 660 patrons in six (freshly carpeted) boutique cinemas. Each Art Deco cinema has its own character and a suitably splendid name like La Scala – complete with comfy, double, leather couches – or the Grand, with its historic Wurlitzer pipe organ that's played on special occasions.

There's leg room aplenty and you can enjoy a glass of wine or two during the show. But the best thing? Even better than all that Deco glamour? There's *no advertising* – just a couple of trailers and it's on to the main event.

> HIT THE STREETS

8 Ballarat St, Yarraville
(03) 9362 0999
www.suntheatre.com.au
Open Mon–Sun (session times vary)

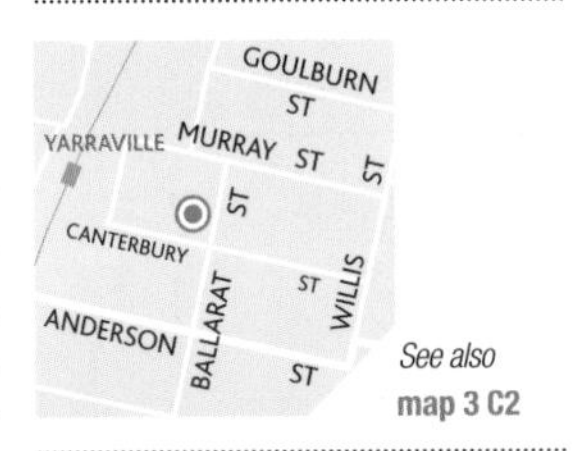

See also **map 3 C2**

'ENCYCLO' TRIVIA

* Art Deco refers to a variety of architectural and design styles that flourished in the early 20th century. At its height, it married function and modernity with style and glamour. One of the most famous examples of an Art Deco building is New York City's Empire State Building.

> HIT THE STREETS

NOT A STITCH OF LYCRA IN SIGHT

Melbourne is arguably Australia's most bicycle-friendly city. There are bike lanes and paths and parks aplenty, and growing legions of bike tribes to fill them – but none quite as classy as the Frocks on Bikes. A fetching blush of lady riders who like to don their prettiest dresses and ride about town in the height of velo-dramatic style, the Frockers – and their bikes – embark on outings anywhere from four to six times a year.

This delightful excuse for a jolly good day out was the brainchild of two Kiwi sheilas who like to dress nice. Melbourne was the first Australian chapter of Frocks on Bikes, and Perth looks set to follow. We can only imagine that with cycle smarts as sartorially elegant as these, there will be more to come.

Fancy a leisurely ride along the St Kilda Foreshore, with an ice-cream at day's end? Perhaps a meander along Merri Creek to sample baked goods from the Abbotsford Convent? A Sunday afternoon of two-wheeled shopping on a Garage Sale Trail, perhaps? Or a winding ride through the backstreets of the inner north to a secret spot where croquet and Pimm's await?

We're all a-quiver at the thought of what the Frockers might have in store for us come Frocktober*. In the meantime, suitably dressed newcomers are always welcome, and well-clad gents are also invited (frocks *not* compulsory). Participation is free. But true style? Priceless.

> HIT THE STREETS

Around and about in Melbourne
www.frocksonbikes.wordpress.com/melbourne
Email frocksonbikes.melbourne@gmail.com for notification of upcoming events

'ENCYCLO' TRIVIA

* Frocktober is an Australian charity initiative that raises money to support the Ovarian Cancer Research Foundation. Participants are required to wear a frock every day for the month of October.

> HIT THE STREETS

YOGA WITH A TWIST

Yoga is a wonderful thing, but it can sometimes take itself a little too seriously for my liking. Namaste* this and happy smiling face that … Just last week I had my head so far up my own asana*, I had trouble seeing the free-range wood from the hand-reared trees.

Finding a class to keep me on my yoga-loving toes is no easy task – but breathe deeply, yogis! I've found a class that will get your chakras* humming, and it's taught by a yogi with her feet firmly planted in the modern world: Melbourne's very own Jo Stewart. She bends, she blogs, she downward dogs*!

Inspired by a dynamic, flowing form of yoga called Vinyasa*, Jo and her music-loving husband Rane have melded their passions for ambient electronica, yoga and good times into a soul-tingling, heart-opening class at the Dance of Life Centre of Yoga and Healing. Each week Jo picks a theme – fire, say, or earth – and Rane creates an accompanying playlist. With names like 'Deep Twitch' or 'Hip-Hop Hips', this fun-loving duo's creations will have you busting a funky frog, putting an extra curl in your cobra and striking a particularly graceful pigeon pose in the blink of an all-seeing eye.

Classes are suitable for all levels, there's plenty of relaxation time on the mat, and sometimes Jo even posts Rane's yogi-licious mixes on her website to download. Now you don't get that at an ashram in the middle of India, do you? See you on the mat.

> HIT THE STREETS

Room 2, Dance of Life,
250 George St, Fitzroy
www.gardenofyoga.com.au/vinyasaplaylist
Classes Mon 7.15–8.45pm

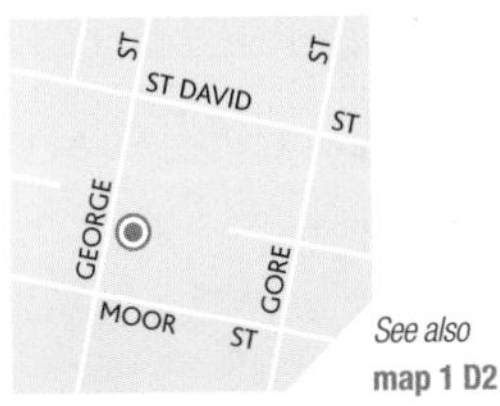

See also **map 1 D2**

'ENCYCLO' TRIVIA

* A common greeting in India, namaste has many translations in English, but it loosely means, 'I honour the divinity within you'.

* Asana is a Sanskrit word used to refer to a yoga pose.

* Chakras are energy centres or centres of spiritual power within the body.

* The downward-facing dog, frog, cobra and pigeon are all bendy-flexy yoga poses.

* Indeed, Vinyasa is often called 'Vinyasa flow' or just 'flow' because you move seamlessly from one asana to the next.

FOOTSCRAY
COMMUNITY
ARTS CENTRE

FOOTSCRAY COMMUNITY ARTS CENTRE

WAY-OUT WEST

Perhaps best known as the backdrop for notorious skinhead flick *Romper Stomper*, Footscray's once-industrial Maribyrnong foreshore has come a long way since then, that's for sure. What's leading the charge? The all-singing, all-dancing Footscray Community Arts Centre!

Put it this way: when the ultra-hip St Jerome's Laneway Festival outgrew the CBD, FCAC was the logical choice for its relocation – that outdoor amphitheatre is pretty special, after all. Special too is the centre's emphasis on community involvement, particularly when it comes to nurturing local talent. Whether it's an exhibition by a promising young artist-in-residence, or a gig showcasing hot new bands from the area, FCAC is plugged in to what's happening in the western suburbs *now*. You never know: you might just discover the next big thing while you're here.

Given the ethnic diversity of Melbourne's west, multicultural events comprise a fair whack of the centre's schedule. Offerings such as Pacific Islander film nights, Indigenous comedy and African photographic exhibitions mean you can take a trip around the world without leaving town. Inclusiveness extends in other directions too with the occasional queer show and a special program for people with disabilities. Like a microcosmic social utopia, everyone is welcome and encouraged to get involved.

Factor in a roster of creative courses and workshops (Hip-Hop Academy, anyone?), and you've got a buzzing cultural hub that not only offers an appealing diversion from the usual inner-city gallery circuit, but comes with river views and an on-site cafe* to boot! Who says you can't have it all?

> HIT THE STREETS

45 Moreland St, Footscray
(03) 9362 8888
footscrayarts.com
Reception open Tues–Fri 9.30am–5pm, Sat–Sun 10am–4pm; check website for event times

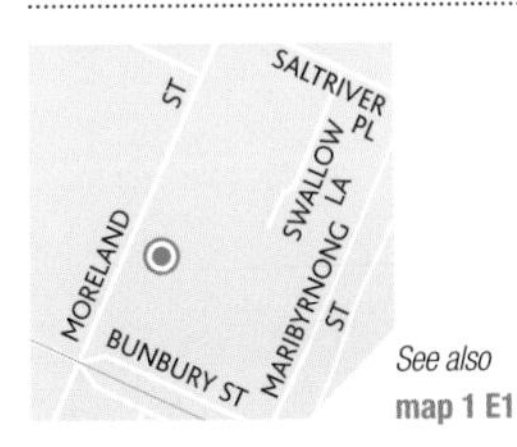

See also **map 1 E1**

'ENCYCLO' TRIVIA

* The popular Happy River Cafe features in *Hide & Seek Melbourne: Feeling Peckish?*

> HIT THE STREETS

RICKETTS POINT MARINE SANCTUARY

WHAT LIES BENEATH

Whoever said appearances can be deceiving might have been talking about Ricketts Point. With its hardy coastal scrub and coarse, greyish-brown sand, this Port Phillip beach ain't exactly Noosa. But set foot in the water, and its charms reveal themselves quick-smart.

Yes, Ricketts Point is all about submerged delights. It's about algae-carpeted rockpools and lush seagrass, enough fish to make your head spin* and armies of small crustaceans. A vibrant universe unto itself, this 115-hectare haven positively hums with life. Say g'day to an eagle ray, wink at a winkle and smile at a sea sponge – you've always got company at Ricketts Point.

But it wasn't always this way. When the state government declared it a sanctuary in 2002, Ricketts Point was on the brink of exhaustion. Decades of relentless shell-fishing had trashed its delicate ecosystem, and many resident critters were dying out. Thankfully, all forms of fishing are now outlawed and the underwater party is booming once more.

The diversity of marine life on display will amaze you, whether you're snorkelling the shallows or exploring the offshore reef and underwater caves. You might even spot a visiting pod of bottlenose dolphins on your travels. Happier on dry land? Expect to make some new feathered friends – the birdlife here is almost as prolific as the aquatic population.

A beachside cafe and some interesting Indigenous history complete the picture, making this an idyllic day out all round. And best of all? Ricketts Point is an easy 20 km from the CBD. Last one in's a rotten sea snail!*

> HIT THE STREETS

Beach Rd, Beaumaris
13 1963 (Parks Victoria Information Centre)
parkweb.vic.gov.au/explore/parks/ricketts-point-marine-sanctuary
Open all hours, but high tide is recommended

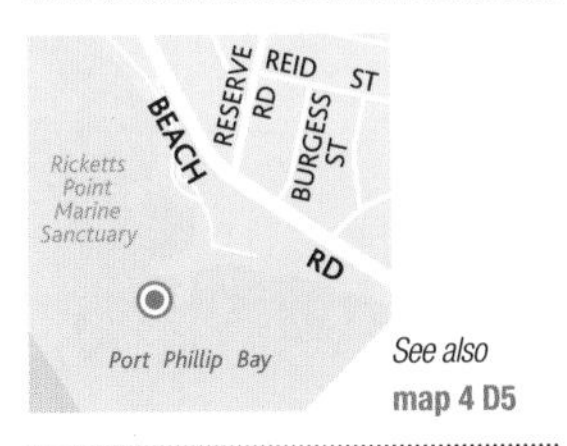

See also **map 4 D5**

'ENCYCLO' TRIVIA

* No less than 51 species of fish have been observed here.

* For the record, Ricketts Point is home to plenty of sea snails too!

Charlie's

TREASURE TROVE

> TREASURE TROVE

DEJOUR JEANS

PERFECT FIT, PERFECT PRICE

Some people are the lucky ones of the denim world. They're the people who can walk into a store, pick a pair of jeans off the rack, check the measurements on the waistband and walk out secure in the knowledge that those new jeans will look stunning on them. Those who aren't so lucky often resort to desperate measures: buying only a single beloved brand, rolling up the leg bottoms or taking them to their long-suffering mothers for alteration. If you're one of the lucky ones, Dejour Jeans' biggest attraction is price. But if you're one of the unlucky ones? Well, your luck's just changed.

Dejour Jeans' premise is simple: affordable, high-quality, custom-tailored jeans. Or, to put it another way, the perfect pair of jeans every time, and at downright decent prices. Owner Nam or one of his assistants will guide you through the available range of colours and styles (these change frequently, so check back if you can't find what you're after the first time). Once you have a prospective new pair of jeans on, Nam will appraise them with a critical eye and recommend alterations if necessary. And maybe you'd like them to be narrower at the ankles, or shorter in the legs. Either way, a crack team of tailors will perform the alterations in around 15 minutes.

And now for the thing we've all been waiting for: the price ... Depending on the style, a pair ranges from around $40 to $55, including any alterations. It's pretty nice up here in the lucky people's world, huh?

> TREASURE TROVE

542 Sydney Rd, Brunswick
(03) 9380 4884
Open Mon–Fri 9.30am–5.30pm, Sat–Sun 10am–5pm

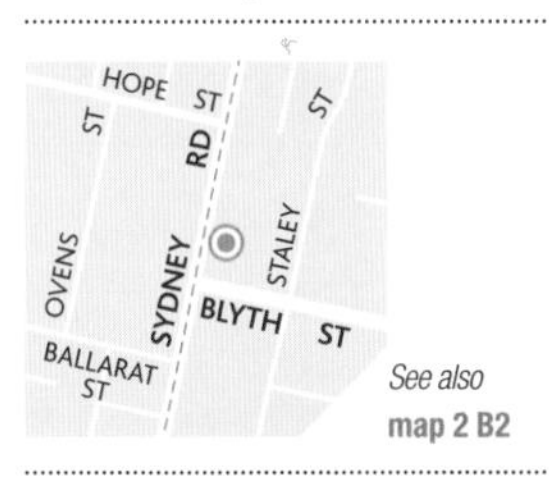

See also **map 2 B2**

HP
WOOLY BULLY
SAM THE SHAM AND THE PHARAOHS
WOOLY BULLY
RECORDS COMICS COFFEE
ROBERT HAZARD
Second hand LPs

COMICS, CASSETTES AND CAFFEINE

Any shop that stocks a comic book called *Mauled: True Stories of People Attacked at the Zoo** has obviously got something, ahem, special going on. When the same shop also sells vinyl records and – gasp! – cassette tapes, but draws the line at CDs, it starts to look even more intriguing. And when you throw in a cafe and occasional gig into the bargain? Well! Then you've really hit the jackpot … Take a bow, Wooly Bully.

Named after the classic '60s stomper by Sam the Sham & the Pharaohs*, this quirky joint is a neighbourhood favourite, beloved by the skinny-jeans set and long-time locals alike. And no wonder: a visit to Wooly Bully is like an instant happy hit. If the candy-coloured, 'retro-tastic' decor doesn't make you smile, the cheerfully subversive range of underground and downright kooky comics certainly will, as will the racks of beautiful, 'browseable' albums and singles, mainly of the garage, punk, pop and psychedelic persuasions. With new stuff arriving every week, you've got the perfect excuse to keep returning too. (And yes, it stocks Sam the Sham – you can even worship at a mini-shrine dedicated to the band if the mood takes you.)

Though recent stats suggest that global sales of vinyl are increasing while CDs do a *Titanic*, the friendly folks at Wooly Bully aren't resting on their laurels. To make customers even happier, they also run a cafe on site, with a small-but-perfect menu of bagels, baguettes, fair-trade coffee and dreamy pastries as tasty as anything on the Errol Street circuit.

Don't be fooled by its modest size. Wooly is mammoth!

> TREASURE TROVE

104 Errol St, North Melbourne
www.woolybully.com.au
Open Tues–Thurs 10am–3pm,
Fri 10am–6pm, Sat–Sun 10am–5pm
(opening hours vary, so check the website for the latest)

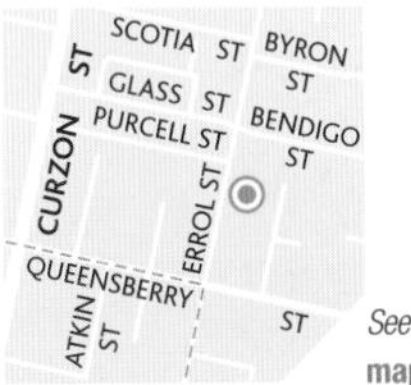

See also **map 1 A2**

'ENCYCLO' TRIVIA

* Including one about the time an ill-advised Sharon Stone arranged for her lizard-loving husband to go inside the komodo dragon enclosure at LA Zoo …

* During the mid-'60s, the fun, catchy songs of Sam the Sham & the Pharaohs packed dance floors around the world. With its hip-shaking rhythm and nonsensical lyrics, their 1965 hit 'Wooly Bully' sealed their legendary status for good.

> TREASURE TROVE

SO:ME SPACE

A MARKET WITHIN A MAZE WITHIN A MARKET

If you do what I did and plunge head first into the organised chaos that is the South Melbourne Market, you might have trouble finding this mini-market within SMM's bounds. Like me, you'll likely wander like a mouse in a particularly eye-catching maze (vegetables! cheese! loaves! fish!) until you stumble across a sign pointing to SO:ME Space at the northern end of aisle E. From here, you'll go up some stairs and end up in the carpark, where you'll adopt a bemused expression and wander from pillar to post like someone who can't remember where they parked their Prius*.

The trick is to go past (not up, you dig?) the aforementioned stairs, where you'll find a softly lit, timber-lined grotto that's home to SO:ME Space. Here, hip young things make, source and sell hip fun things – think locally designed shoes, skincare products and vintage collectables. Permanent stall holders ring the outside, while less permanent pop-ups occupy the central space.

One of our favourite stalls is One Little Piggie, a curated bookstore stocking new, classic and limited-edition tomes to make your eyes fill with happy tears. Another is the Bakerlite Trading Company, which sells Pashley* bicycles and accessories, along with chichi helmets, saddle bags, scooters and other aesthetically adroit items to beautify your bicycling life. Then there's Stone Glint & Bone, Emma Luke's drool-inducing jewellery collective, and Mr Simple, creator of stylish threads for blokes. And there's more. Much, much more. Plus, SO:ME Space is open on Thursday nights, while the rest of the South Melbourne Market slumbers – which should, in theory, make it that little bit easier to find.

> TREASURE TROVE

South Melbourne Market, cnr Coventry & Cecil sts (enter from Cecil St), South Melbourne
(03) 9209 6295
www.somespace.com.au
Open Wed & Sat–Sun 9am–4pm, Thurs 5–9pm, Fri 9am–5pm

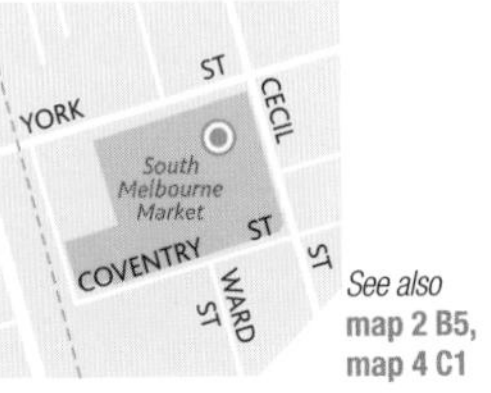

See also **map 2 B5, map 4 C1**

'ENCYCLO' TRIVIA

* A Prius is Toyota's eco-friendly car model, which uses 'hybrid' technology (the car is powered through both a petrol engine and electric motor). American politician turned environmental activist Al Gore is a big fan of this car.

* Pashley is a British company that's been hand-building bicycles in Stratford-upon-Avon since 1926. The Bakerlite Trading Company is Victoria's sole trader of these beautiful bikes.

The Good Brew Co.
www.thegoodbrew.com.au

THE GOOD BREW COMPANY

GREEN-FRIENDLY CATERING CO.

The aftermath of a good party or festival is always severe. How many times have you left a gig or great night out having to step over piles of discarded plastic cups, empty bottles and other trash? It's the environmental equivalent of the walk of shame. And according to the Good Brew Company, it's completely unnecessary.

Dean O'Callaghan, an easygoing, affable chap and Good Brew's owner, is devoted to finding the happy medium between good beer and good karma. After some time overseas, he returned to Australia dreaming of making a difference to the environmental hangover of a good night out. Sure, cans and bottles can be recycled (and most venues and punters usually have the best intentions), but Good Brew takes it up a notch.

No need for a truck to deliver your kegs, or car trips to the bottle shop throughout the night when you have Deano delivering straight to you on his specialised cargo bike. Who needs to separate paper and plastic for recycling at the end of the night when all the cups are made from sustainable bamboo? Even the bar set-up supplied for you and your crew is packaging free, and all beers and other drinks provided are sourced from environmentally friendly breweries that have a focus on sustainability. Everybody wins.

So keep Dean and his brewing crew in mind for your next Melbourne function. Your guests, your belly and your planet will thank you.

> TREASURE TROVE

Deliveries available within the CBD and some inner Melbourne suburbs
0430 290 952
www.goodbrew.com.au

MAGIC LANTERN STUDIO

CLEVER CURIOSITIES FROM YESTERYEAR

Do you ever wonder what your great-great-grandfather might have bought your great-great-grandmother when they were courting back in the day? A trip to Fitzroy's Magic Lantern Studio might give you some idea. This pint-sized house of wonder is bursting with pre-cinematic technology, curiosities and ephemera from yesteryear – the kinds of novelties that would have made great-great-grandmother Gertie gasp with delight, and wonder what else her charming beau might have up his sleeve.

Nestled in an old bluestone building next to a laundromat, Magic Lantern is the love child of Argentinean gentleman Gonzalo Varela and his beautiful and artistic wife, Lucy Parkinson. They have an amazing eye for treasures from times gone by and sell clever figments of the imagination – curious things you've never heard of like thaumatropes* and praxinoscopes*. Other gems include old-fashioned light boxes, miniature Victorian-style theatres, dreamily surrealist paintings made by Lucy, eerily lifelike puppets from the Czech Republic, and other handmade puppets straight from the mind of Gonzalo himself. There are even – as this studio, playroom and shop's name would suggest – magic lanterns* for sale, and an in-house theatre for puppet shows is on the agenda.

This delightfully arty and quirky store has as many aspects as a kaleidoscope has patterns. It's magical and mad and other-worldly, enough to make *all* children – that's proper, school-going nippers as well as grown-up kids with jobs and mortgages – feel enchanted. It's a happily-ever-after kind of place that would've tickled Gertie and her beau a particularly pleasing shade of pink.

> TREASURE TROVE

155 Brunswick St, Fitzroy
www.magiclanternstudio.com
Open Wed–Sat 11am–6pm

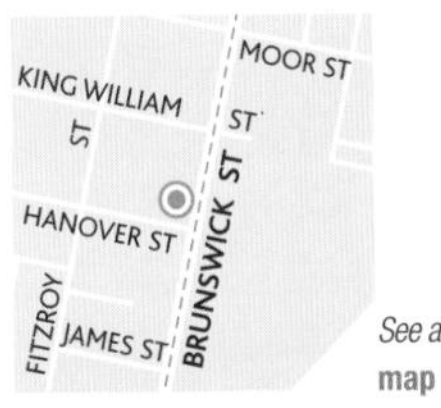

See also **map 1 D3**

'ENCYCLO' TRIVIA

* A thaumatrope is a disc with two different pictures on each side that, when spun, creates a single image.

* A praxinoscope is an early animation device made of a strip of pictures placed around the inner surface of a spinning, mirrored cylinder.

* A magic lantern is a pre-cinematic, gas- or flame-powered image projector developed in the 17th century.

> TREASURE TROVE

FLYING THE FLAG FOR OLD-SCHOOL COOL

So you feel a Liz Taylor moment coming on, but your wardrobe's vibing more Joey Ramone*. Do you:

a) Get on eBay and bid for the first vintage dress you find, crossing your fingers it'll fit?

b) Give up, flop on the couch and watch *Butterfield 8**?

or

c) Make tracks to Frocks and Slacks?

Ask any local vintage buff and they'll tell you it's Frocks and Slacks all the way, baby. This cult boutique has been keeping fans of bygone times looking sharp in the finest vintage clothing and accessories for almost 15 years, and offers a chic, affordable alternative for anyone averse to mainstream, trend-driven fashion.

As any Barkly Street habitué would know, Frocks and Slacks' ever-changing, colour-themed and artfully arranged window displays are an attraction in themselves. Step inside and the effect is magnified. Welcome to a vibrant world where black is just a supporting actor to a headline cast of vivid pinks, greens, blues, yellows and oranges. Where flamboyant Hawaiian shirts jostle with preloved jackets for your attention, and a cabinet bursting with marvellous jewellery beckons. Where frocks and slacks are just the beginning …

All stock is personally sourced by owner Tracy, who knows what's on the shelves at any time down to the last item. Going to a '20s theme party? She'll find you an outfit. Allergic to synthetic fabrics? Try something in cotton or cashmere. So head down to Frocks and Slacks, and don't slack off about frocking up a minute longer!

> TREASURE TROVE

188E Barkly St, St Kilda
(03) 9537 2337
www.facebook.com/pages/Frocks-and-Slacks/130409413678476
Open Mon–Sun 10.30am–6.30pm

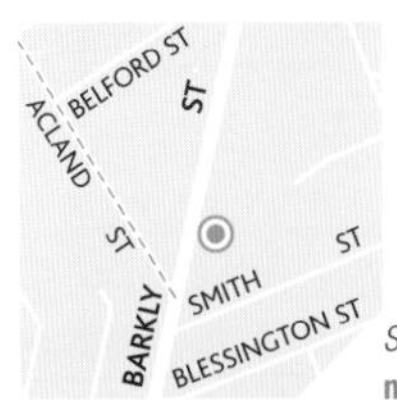

See also **map 4 D4**

'ENCYCLO' TRIVIA

* Former front man of legendary New York punk band The Ramones, Joey Ramone was not known for his fine threads, generally preferring an ensemble of scruffy jeans, T-shirt and leather jacket.

* *Butterfield 8* is a 1960 film in which Elizabeth Taylor played the role of a glamorous Manhattan girl about town.

Yarraville

WE HEART YARRAVILLE

Yarraville's a unique suburb, even by Melbourne standards. Despite being ringed by arterial roads and heavy industry, the suburb's beating heart – known as 'the village' to locals – feels less like a suburb and more like a small country town. It's the kind of place where it only takes two visits to a cafe before you no longer have to give your name for your takeaway flat white. So it's no surprise that Yarraville's coolest gift and clothing boutique, Village Idiom, likes keeping things local.

How local? Well, how about Nicola Cerini handbags, manufactured mere kilometres from the store, giving them a tiny carbon footprint? Or, if you prefer, leather satchels from Peter O'Connor, resident leatherworker in Melbourne's iconic Nicholas Building*? Or a funky, locally made clock? Or jewellery that owner Alexis Ensor first spotted on a young Yarraville lass who just happened to be starting her own jewellery business around the corner?

You might be detecting a theme here. Yes, wherever possible, Village Idiom sticks to locally produced, low-volume and environmentally sustainable goods. Its commendable commitment to these ethics doesn't mean that there's no sense of fun here, though – quite the contrary. The store's overriding aesthetic is one of contemporary kitsch. A rich stew of idiosyncratic cultural references sees Mexican calaveras* bump up against Russian matryoshka dolls* filled with ever-smaller versions of Lady Gaga. Village life has never been so wackily cosmopolitan.

> TREASURE TROVE

34 Anderson St, Yarraville
(03) 9687 3445
www.villageidiom.com.au
Open Mon–Fri 10am–6pm,
Sat 10am–5pm, Sun 11am–4pm

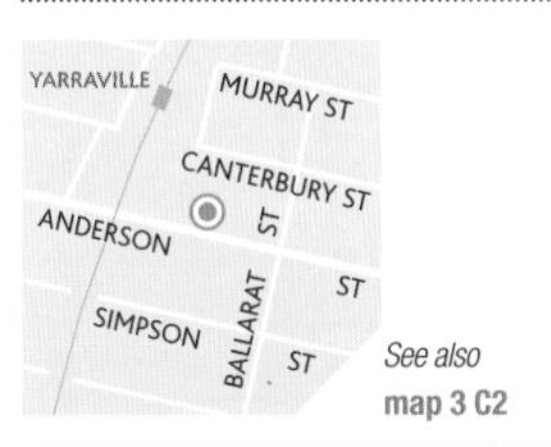

See also **map 3 C2**

'ENCYCLO' TRIVIA

* The Nicholas Building, on the corner of Flinders Lane and Swanston Street in Melbourne's CBD, is a much-loved warren of artists' studios.

* Calaveras are the skeletal forms associated with Mexico's Día de los Muertos, or Day of the Dead, made popular by the satirical cartoons of José Guadalupe Posada.

* Matryoshka is the Russian word for the famous wooden dolls that stack neatly inside each other.

French
Modern Vintag
THE

PATCHWORK ON CENTRAL PARK

GET YOUR GRANDMA ON

I've lived around the corner from Patchwork on Central Park my whole life, but I've never been inside before now. Why? Because from the outside it looks suspiciously as if the inside might be filled with old women who live with (and talk to) their dozens of cats.

Once inside though, I was simply blown away. The brightly coloured fabrics dazzled me with their stunning patterns and textures, as did the selection of vintage-inspired themes and Japanese designs. Haberdashery-esque thingamabobs and whatsits abound, and I could've spent a happy couple of hours simply exploring this beautiful and fascinating space. For me, Patchwork on Central Park epitomises what my nanna's attic should have been like. Rolls of trims stacked high? Check. Buckets of notions*, knick-knacks and quilting patches scattered everywhere? Absolutely. Drawers and bookcases filled to the brim with fabrics, bobbles and spools of thread? You bet.

Patchwork takes the art of quilting seriously, offering over ten different types of quilting and patchworking classes, as well as a cushion-making class. Much more than just a shop where you stock up on sewing supplies, it's also a place where you can socialise with others with similar interests, swap patterns or simply find some time for yourself.

If you get parched from all of your sewing and shopping, just a few doors away is Our Kitchen Table, an inviting, homely place (much like nanna's) where you can partake of something savoury or sweet accompanied by tea in an old china cup.

Ladies, it's time to celebrate your inner grandma.

> TREASURE TROVE

148 Burke Rd, East Malvern
(03) 9885 4480
www.patchworkoncentralpark.com.au
Open Mon–Fri 10am–4.30pm,
Sat 10am–4pm, Sun 12–4pm

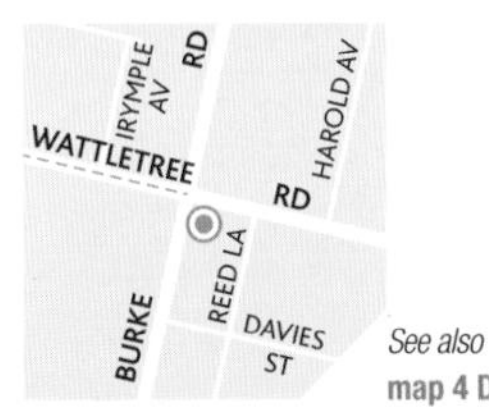

See also **map 4 D4**

'ENCYCLO' TRIVIA

* A notion is a tool or device to help you sew.

> TREASURE TROVE

ART WITHOUT ATTITUDE

Let's face it: if you're after a good, affordable piece of art, visiting a traditional gallery probably isn't the best idea. They're great to look around, sure, but buying anything can necessitate taking out a second mortgage. Signed & Numbered, however, breaks the mould of the quiet, stuffy, over-priced gallery. You're sure to find something here that is both easy on the eye, and the pocket.

But it's the informality and unpretentiousness that sets Signed & Numbered even further apart. This small gallery-slash-shop feels more like an active artist's studio, which helps to break down the barrier between artist and buyer that can be felt in stuffier galleries. There's certainly no fear of having someone look down their nose at you here! On the contrary, gallery owner Jacqui Vidal is more than happy to chat, even if she's in the middle of framing a customer's purchase.

Vidal was inspired by a tiny Parisian shop that sold art in hard-backed sleeves displayed in crates like albums in a record shop. Which leads to another point of difference – there's not much art hanging on the walls of this intimate space. Rather, gallery goers are encouraged to flick casually through the crates of limited-edition prints from mostly Australian and some international artists. The works span everything from fine art to street art, and all, of course, are signed by the artist and numbered.

Vidal attributes the success of Signed & Numbered to the fact that she followed her heart – all the way back from Paris. One thing's for sure: it's still leading her in the right direction.

> TREASURE TROVE

135 Greville St, Prahran
0413 921 046
www.signedandnumbered.com.au
Open Tues–Fri 11am–5pm,
Sat 10am–5pm, Sun 11am–4pm

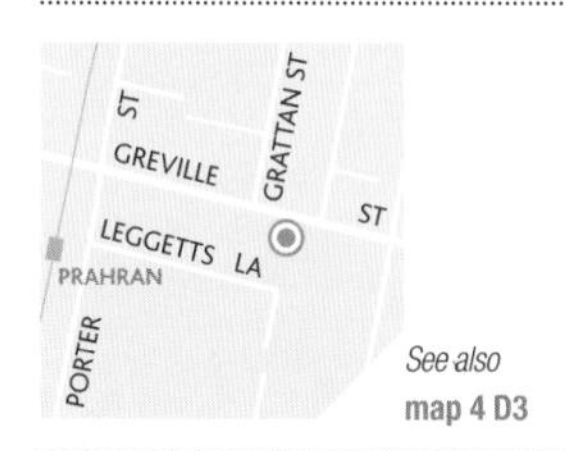

See also **map 4 D3**

> **TREASURE TROVE**

SHELLEY PANTON

MIDDLE PARK MIRAGE

Middle Park may seem safe and genteel, but be warned! You need to keep your wits about you, because lurking in the backstreets of this sleepy suburb is a woman who likes to throw pots! But don't worry, she's not dangerous. She's artisan potter Shelley Panton and the only thing she's crazy for is crockery.

Her studio/shop is surprisingly located in a quiet street, tucked among splendid houses and apartments. Inside Shelley Panton (the shop) you'll find Shelley Panton (the work) alongside other creations by Melbourne artists, arranged in a colour-coded sea of pastels. And, if you're lucky, Shelley Panton (the woman) will be behind her potter's wheel. You can chat with Shelley as you browse this vision splendid of everything for the table and home: think kitchen linen, lamps, frames, arty books, soft furnishings, stationery, candles, gourmet pantry staples, and, of course, pottery. While some things may be out of your price range, others cost as little as $6. In any case, you can look for free.

Everything for sale is so beautiful, you'll wish this was your home – and for a night you can pretend it is at one of Shelley's quarterly dinner parties. A top Melbourne chef does the cooking, a local vigneron serves the wine, Shelley's crockery adorns the table, and other artists share their crafts over an intimate dinner for 24. It's a truly magical evening – without a smashed dinner plate or bowl in sight.

> TREASURE TROVE

88 Park Rd, Middle Park
(03) 9537 0737
www.shelleypanton.com
Open Wed–Sat 10am–5.30pm, Sun 10am–4pm (Mon–Tues by appointment)

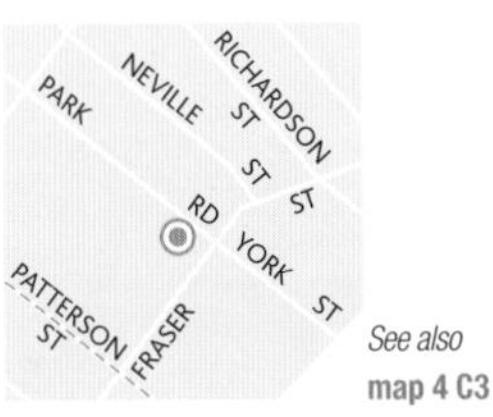

See also **map 4 C3**

FEELING PECKISH?

> FEELING PECKISH?

ELCEED, EL MAGNÍFICO!

Has anyone else noticed how North Melbourne seems to sprout new cafes at a rate matched only by a rabbit's reproductive output? You'd think it would've reached saturation point by now. But if the lovely and loveable Elceed* is any indication, this happening 'hood is still hitting the caffeinated heights.

Occupying premises that once housed a dingy Italian coffee den, Elceed easily holds its own amid some illustrious neighbours. Breezy and friendly, with loads of space (including a sunny courtyard out back) and an open kitchen, it's the kind of place you'll want to share with friends and family – over and over again.

Indeed, what better way to get fully acquainted with the menu? With an emphasis on brunch fare like bruschetta, baked eggs and granola, Elceed takes these tried-and-true classics and gives them a sassy makeover. The eggs are baked differently each day (the cauliflower-and-béchamel variation is to die for), while the mushroom bruschetta dazzles with its delirious mix of goat's-cheese feta, candied prosciutto and olive tapenade. As for the raspberry-and-almond-topped rice pudding, two words suffice – ye gods!

And that's before you've even tried the coffee. The gang here knows its beans, and uses tasty Melbourne-roasted Supreme, guaranteed to kick-start your heart. The funky vintage decor, on the other hand, will lift your spirits. Pulled together with shoestring genius by owner Hannah and her partner Bill, the vibrant tangerine-and-violet colour scheme and myriad cute details* combine to create an infectiously cheery vibe that could brighten the darkest day. Elceed? Yes please!

> FEELING PECKISH?

610 Queensberry St, North Melbourne
(03) 9326 8648
Open Tues–Fri 7am–4pm, Sat 8am–4pm

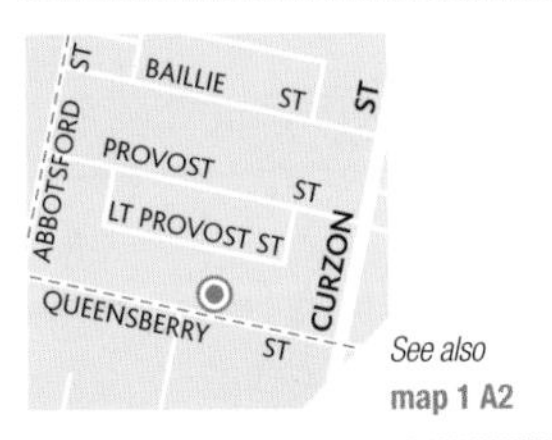

See also **map 1 A2**

'ENCYCLO' TRIVIA

* Alcide from *True Blood*, or El Cid, the medieval Spanish military legend? The name for this cafe was inspired by both these powerful characters.

* Cute details include psychedelic owl murals on the toilet doors and groovy retro wallpaper in the front room (put up by Hannah's mum, no less).

GUMBO
PO' BOY -
DEEP FRIED OYSTER
FRIED SHRIMP
BEEF DEBRIS
THE DOM -
CHUNKY FRIES
SODAS
WATER
GUMBO
KITCHEN

GUMBO KITCHEN

TOE-TAPPING FINGER-LICKIN' FUN

Melbourne's gone a little bit nuts for food trucks of late, and there's one in particular that's causing a stir: the Gumbo Kitchen. This blue-and-white dream machine, run by Michael Cotter and Patricia Stanton, serves New Orleans–inspired Creole* and Cajun* food. Here's Michael and Patricia's recipe for a mighty fine meal:

Tune in (to the web, Facebook, Twitter) for the word on where Gumbo Kitchen is parking next. Arrive. Bring an appetite and pull up a picnic blanket: Gumbo provides these, gratis. Step up to the window. Order. Now here's where it starts getting tricky, folks, but rest assured, *you cannot make a bad choice*.

I opt for the po'boy, a submarine sandwich swimming with deep-fried shrimp, lettuce, tomato, pickles and spicy mayo. Sometimes it'll come with beef instead of shrimp – either way it's a little bit lively, a little bit chunky and a lot of delicious. You may go for gumbo instead. Wise choice; it's one heck of a dish. A meat-based stew-cum-soup, it includes celery, bell peppers and onions (a culinary partnership known as the 'holy trinity' in Cajun cuisine). There's a smattering of other dishes to choose from, including vegetarian options. And for dessert – lemon ice box pie*, anyone?

For optimum mouth parties, we recommend chewing your food in time with the truck's Dixie* music: the snare drum's ra-ta-ta-ta and the tuba's pom-pom-pa will have you ready for seconds in no time. Hot diggity dog!

> FEELING PECKISH?

Various locations, especially north-side
www.gumbokitchen.com
Open for lunch & dinner some time, somewhere, most days of the week

'ENCYCLO' TRIVIA

* Creole people are of Native American, African American and colonial (especially French and Spanish) descent. Creole cuisine blends the flavours of their countries of origin with local ingredients.

* Cajun people are descendants of the Acadians of French Canada. Their cuisine arose from the adaptation of simple, rustic, provincial French cooking to local ingredients.

* Lemon ice box pie is a heavenly frozen pie made from lemon juice, lots of eggs, sweetened condensed milk and other yummy things.

* Dixie is a style of jazz that developed in New Orleans at the start of the 20th century.

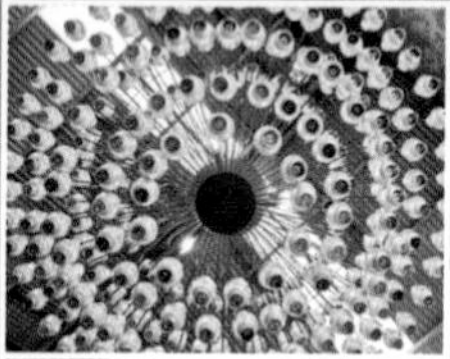

MIDDLE FISH

THAI THIS ON FOR SIZE

If Seven Seeds* put the otherwise unremarkable Berkeley Street on the map, then Middle Fish – located in a converted warehouse next door – has sealed the deal. In a city of fickle foodies tirelessly chasing their next culinary kick, this airy new Thai cafe has already attracted a loyal following. Your first hint that Middle Fish is no ordinary Thai eatery is the metallic chandelier presiding over the entrance. Several eye-popping, specially commissioned pieces by Chiang Mai artist Torlarp Larpjaroensook confirm this impression (as does the conspicuous absence of heavy golden cutlery!). Seating options range from inviting booths and couches to stools at the front window. It's a huge space, with an exuberant, modern vibe.

The menu, however, is grounded in tradition, focusing on authentic southern Thai cuisine. Prepared with fresh market-bought ingredients, regional favourites like massaman curry*, tom yum* and spicy salads are served up so quickly that the veggies are still crunchy and the meat literally sizzling. Can't decide what to order? Try the tom kha: seriously, the exquisite flavours in this fragrant coconut soup will set your tastebuds a-tango. Adventurous brunchers also have much to celebrate, starting with the blissful banana roti with sweetened condensed milk. Sure, it's not highfalutin gastronomy, but it *is* drop-dead delicious – and that's what counts. (Well, that and the fact that all mains cost less than $20.)

Owners Pla, a Thai expat, and David have put a lot of love into Middle Fish, and it shows. The service is friendly, the servings are generous and the customers always seem to be smiling. Kŏr hâi jà-rern aa-hăan!*

> FEELING PECKISH?

122–128 Berkeley St, Carlton
(03) 9348 1704
Open Mon–Fri 7am–5pm,
Sat–Sun 10am–4pm

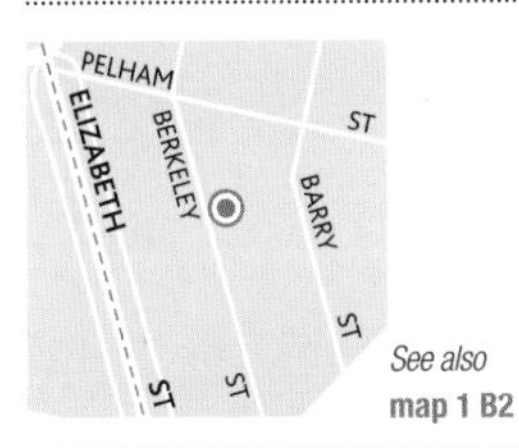

See also
map 1 B2

'ENCYCLO' TRIVIA

* Seven Seeds features in *Hide & Seek Melbourne: Feeling Peckish?*

* Massaman is a mild curry with lots of potato and cashews.

* Tom yum is a tangy, spicy clear soup, popular in Thailand and Laos.

* That's Thai for 'bon appétit', folks!

PREMIUM BAKER'S
FLOUR
PREMIUM BAKER'S
FLOUR
10 KG

AL ALBERO

PIZZA FROM PADDOCK TO PLATE

A chef's got to be pretty confident to have an open-plan restaurant, given that all eyes will be on him as he toils away in the kitchen. Al Albero's Joe Coppini is definitely confident. Diners at his open-plan pizza place can observe him making each pizza from scratch. And we mean from *scratch* – it wouldn't surprise us if there was a goat out the back supplying the main ingredient for the oft-featured goat's-cheese topping.

Yes, things are about as fresh as they come here. Joe creates limited quantities of pizza toppings each day, and once they've sold out? That's it for the day, folks. Equally impressive is the fact that Al Albero's bases are made with biodynamic and organic Australian flour and olive oil, the toppings are organic and locally sourced wherever possible, and the cheeses are handmade by Victorian farmers.

Diners, sitting among precariously stacked crates of fresh vegetables in the smallish space, are treated to such joys as the house special, a vegetarian delight that combines tomato, pumpkin, roasted capsicum and goat's cheese with a bold amount of fresh parsley. Carnivores buckle at the knees for the slow-cooked lamb pizza, featuring braised lamb-shank meat, tomato, goat's cheese and thyme. There's none of that fashionable thin-and-crispy crust going on here; no, Al Albero pizzas come on a deliciously thick, fluffy cloud of lighter-than-air dough, and are best eaten with a knife and fork.

There's a short dessert menu, or you can help yourself to the baskets of fruit provided free for all to enjoy. If you think that's a nice touch, just wait till you wrap your smiling gear around one of those fresh-from-the-paddock pizzas. One bite and you'll understand why chef Joe is so confident.

> FEELING PECKISH?

354 St Georges Rd, North Fitzroy
(03) 9486 3233
Open Mon–Tues 5pm–late,
Wed–Sun 12pm–late

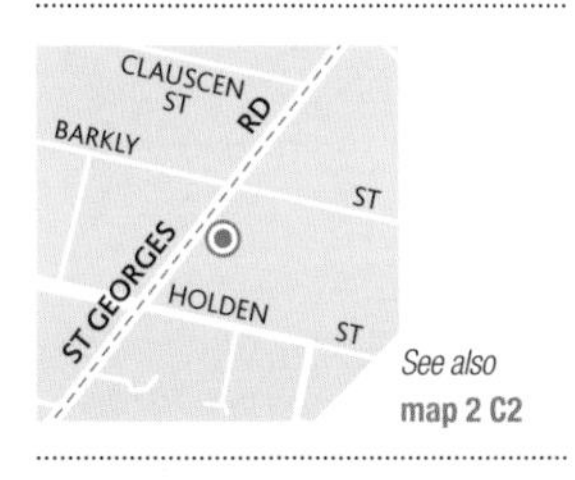

See also **map 2 C2**

JARRITOS
MI CASA
SU CASA

PACIFIC

SEE YA LATER OLD EL PASO

Let's face it: the Mexican food we've become used to in Australia is not much chop ... We don't mean to diss the tacos your mum used to make from an Old El Paso kit, or tarnish cherished memories of giant melted-cheese-laden burritos from your local Tex-Mex joint, but the truth is, there's more to Mexican food than corn chips and cheese.

Lucky for us, then, that local restaurateurs are getting clued into this, and an exciting new wave of Mexican cuisine has hit Melbourne. And while Fonda may not be the first restaurant on the scene to challenge our childhood memories of Mexican food, it's arguably one of the finest (and the best value for money).

The secret to its success? A little leeway in terms of authenticity. You won't see many street vendors in downtown Puerto Vallarta stuffing their burritos with quinoa and kangaroo fillet, but Fonda does, creating a tasty meal that's low in fat and supremely healthy. Other fresh, surprising produce that livens up the menu includes the pea-and-mint combo in the vegetarian taco, and asparagus in one of the quesadillas. But for something more authentic, there are tasty drinks, including Jarritos soda* and horchata* – or, if you fancy a frozen Margarita instead, you can rest assured that the tequila is 100% agave*. Even the bright decor confidently fuses Mexican shabby chic with contemporary Australian minimalism.

This is Mexican with a respectable Aussie twist, but with its feet firmly planted in the mother country's tradition – Fonda is, after all, named after the impromptu restaurants that open in Mexican family homes. Keeping it fresh, healthy and traditional is no mean feat, but Fonda pulls it off with aplomb. ¡Viva!

> FEELING PECKISH?

248 Swan St, Richmond
(03) 9429 0085
www.fondamexican.com.au
Open Sun–Thurs 12–9.30pm, Fri–Sat 12–10.30pm

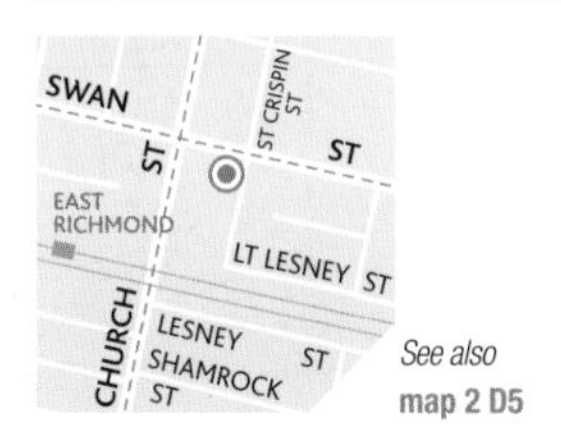

See also **map 2 D5**

'ENCYCLO' TRIVIA

* Jarritos soda is one of the most popular soft-drink brands in Mexico.

* Horchata is a traditional Mexican beverage made from a variety of ingredients. Fonda's horchata combines rice, water, cinnamon, vanilla and evaporated milk.

* Tequila is traditionally made from the agave plant, but many tequilas on the Australian market are 'mixtos' – adulterated with cheap sugar-cane spirit. Tequila made with 100% agave is a superior product, and one that Australians are beginning to appreciate.

DARAC BAR & GRILL

WOULD YOU LIKE SPAM WITH THAT?

Now who'd have thought we'd ever recommend a place where one of the dishes has ingredients including Spam (yes, you read correctly) and Kraft Singles–like processed cheese? Well that's exactly what we're about to do. Korean restaurant Darac Bar & Grill is definitely worthy of your attention – dubious-sounding ingredients notwithstanding.

Nestled under an old brick warehouse on quiet A'Beckett Street, Darac is a lowkey, dimly lit joint, where Korean uni students are the main players (although everyone's welcome, of course). Before you diss the pink excuse for meat that is Spam, it actually adds pizzazz to Darac's Korean Army Stew, gradually reducing down with the soupy stock to a thick, curry-like sauce. The processed cheese also (strangely) makes perfect sense in this dish, which, like other stews and hotpot-style dishes on the menu, you cook yourself on portable gas cookers.

Prefer the chefs in the kitchen to do the cooking? And like your meat real or no deal? Then get it grilled as a steak or skewered on Paddle Pop* sticks for a barbecued delight. There are also soups and tasty gyoza (pan-fried dumplings). Wash it all down with a Korean beer or soju* and you're doing it like the locals. The bar here serves up seriously cheap cocktails too, but there's nothing else serious about them: they're fun, sweet *and* fluorescent.

The decor adds to the unexpected mix with vintage knick-knacks, quirky artworks and Polaroids of posing customers. Word is spreading fast about this hideout, so hotfoot it here before the Spam and plastic cheese run out.

> FEELING PECKISH?

51 A'Beckett St, Melbourne
(03) 9662 2441
Open Mon–Fri 12– 2pm & 6–10pm, Sat 6–10pm

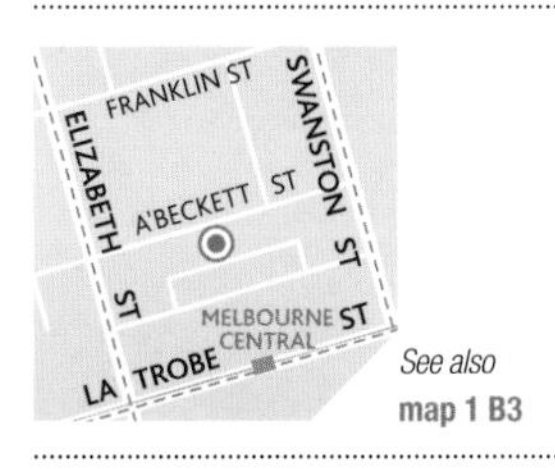

See also **map 1 B3**

'ENCYCLO' TRIVIA

* A Paddle Pop is a well-known Australian ice-cream served on a popsicle stick.

* Soju is a Korean distilled rice liquor, similar to vodka but sweeter.

BACKSTREET CAFE

BRINGING COUNTRY EATS TO THE CITY STREETS

Tim Tehan might be a coffee-brewing, bike-riding, Sunday-paper-reading city slicker now, but he grew up in the country, and, well, it shows. The man pickles his own walnuts, cures his own meats and bakes his own bread. He can skin a rabbit, milk a cow and sweep out a barn – and that's before the sun has even thought about crawling out of bed and staggering to the bathroom to check it's still got its eyebrows.

Lucky for you and me, huh? Because Tehan's latest venture, Backstreet Cafe – a corner cafe, provedore, bakery, charcuterie, restaurant and bar – is all about bringing a little bit of old-school country-food processing and hospitality to city living. Located at the base of an apartment behemoth on a busy bike corridor in the inner north, it looks and tastes like home.

At street level is the cafe, a pavement spiller with a come-hither bar and a buttery-yellow glow. Downstairs? A dungeon-like curing room, where handmade salami hangs and beef ages. In the middle of the room sits a great slab of marble, where patrons can take part in degustation dinners and sausage- and salami-making classes.

The dishes at Backstreet are designed for sharing. We gun for the rabbit, tenderly braised in a sherry, almond and apricot stew, with green and Israeli couscous salads on the side. Then, dessert. I'll take the dark-chocolate torte with beetroot ice-cream, please. Sharing be damned; this one I'm keeping to myself.

> FEELING PECKISH?

152 Kerr St, Fitzroy
(03) 9417 1212
Open Mon–Fri 7am–10.30pm, Sat–Sun 8am–10.30pm

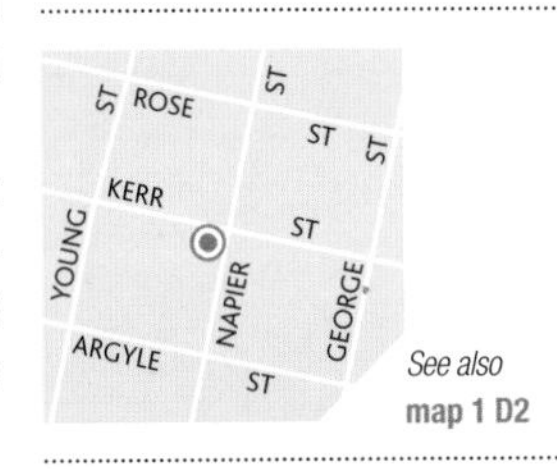

See also **map 1 D2**

LEONARD
COHEN
PAUL KELLY

FAMOUS BLUE RAINCOAT

LEONARD WOULD LOVE IT

First thing's first: where on earth is South Kingsville? Melbourne's west may be undergoing a much-feted cultural and culinary renaissance lately, but this petite enclave near Yarraville seems to have escaped the hype. Strange, considering it's home to the wonderful Famous Blue Raincoat.

Star of the Vernon Street shopping strip, this free-spirited cafe dishes up lashings of warmth and humour along with its hearty meals. It's a bit like visiting your favourite hippy aunt, actually. That is if she lives among comfy couches and eclectic furniture, with colourful paintings and groovin' music on the stereo. This boho-charm extends to the leafy courtyard out back, where a huge floral mural and dozens of pot plants set the scene. Clear your diary, as you'll probably want to linger a while.

Instead of numbers to put on their tables, diners are given toy animals. This whimsical touch seems to work just fine – meals are served promptly and with a smile. Breakfast runs the gamut from classic (bircher muesli) to gourmet (Raincoat Benedictine*) to deliciously naughty (pancakes with bacon and maple syrup). Kids get their own special menu. The extensive lunch and dinner menu is packed with irresistible, budget-friendly options, with the generous share plates being especially good value. The free-range chicken parmigiana, meanwhile, rivals that of any gastro-pub. After something stronger than coffee? Check out FBR's respectable wine list.

Any cafe that's named after a much-loved Leonard Cohen song* is obviously going to have music on the menu too. FBR doesn't disappoint, hosting live jazz, folk and blues acts every Friday night and Sunday afternoon. Cool tunes, great food and good vibes: what more could you possibly want?

> FEELING PECKISH?

25B Vernon St, South Kingsville
(03) 9391 8520
famousblueraincoat.com.au
Open Wed–Sun 9am–11pm

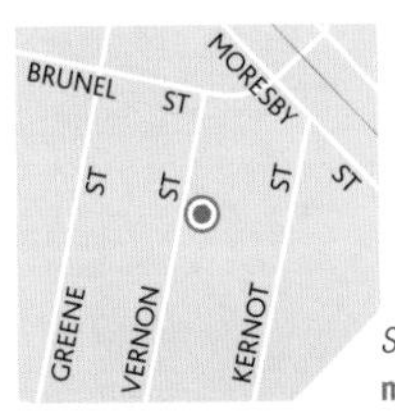

See also **map 3 A4**

'ENCYCLO' TRIVIA

* Raincoat Benedictine is a creative spin on eggs Benedict, with béarnaise sauce instead of hollandaise.

* 'Famous Blue Raincoat' is on Leonard Cohen's 1971 album *Songs of Love and Hate*, and has been covered by everyone from Tori Amos to Joan Baez.

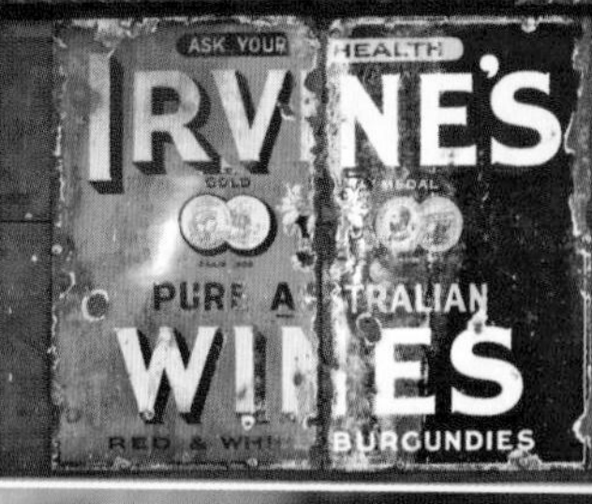

> FEELING PECKISH?

MICHELANGELO

A 30-MINUTE ROMAN HOLIDAY

They say Rome wasn't built in a day, and you know why? Because the Romans were taking a holiday in Melbourne! Only you won't catch the guys behind Michelangelo sleeping on the job – no, they're serving up a storm and showing city workers how to make the most of their 30-minute lunch break.

You really could get used to this. Service is swift, the staff are swoony and oh, the soup! Slow-cooked and flavoursome, just how nonna used to make it. The must-try sourdough bread is handmade out the back every morning; you get it with your soup and, of course, it's in the pizza.

Groups can assemble upstairs around big tables covered with everyone's favourite red-and-white chequered tablecloths. Wall-to-wall dark-wood panelling and well-worn floorboards add to the authentico Italiano feel. You'll find the prime tables up here beside enormous windows fronting leafy Queen Street – a great spot to enjoy the $17 per person sharing menu (two pastas, salad and garlic bread) and the cacophony of happy chatter of the lunchtime crowd that only a genuine Italian restaurant could inspire.

Downstairs is less restaurant, more bar-cafe, with solid slate floors and pictures of the motherland to help you dream away the last minutes of lunch while your gnocchi settles. The natural conclusion to lunch here is coffee – that essential power shot to see you through the afternoon. The current craze in Rome is ginseng coffee, and Michelangelo's owners are running with it. Ginseng is said to boost vitality, so you can imagine the hit when combining it with a double espresso … Those Romans sure don't do things by half.

> FEELING PECKISH?

215 Queen St, Melbourne
(03) 9670 2157
www.michelangelocafe.com.au
Open Mon–Fri 7am–5pm

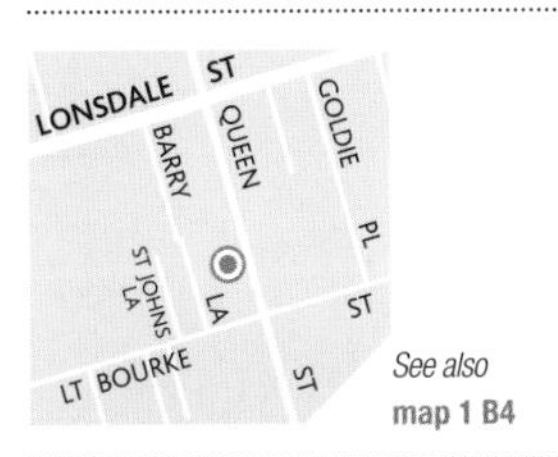

See also **map 1 B4**

Join Shyun's
Membership

SHYUN

LESS YEN, MORE YUM

You've probably heard of the two-step, a groovy little sliding-step manoeuvre used in various dancing genres, from country and western to break-dancing. Well here's a two-step of a different kind, one that'll make your tastebuds have a dance party in your mouth. It's the DIY two-step bento box*, created in – you guessed it – two simple steps, and it's yours for the creating and tasting at Shyun.

A small, unpretentious eatery, Shyun means 'excellence' and 'goodness' in Japanese, but it may as well also mean 'delicious', 'inexpensive' and 'authentic'. For those DIY bento boxes, you choose from a range of dishes to create your own personalised combo. Step one: start with the base $4 price to cover rice and a small salad. Step two: choose two or three dishes that appeal most, each of which cost between just $3 and $5. Ta-da! And there are some great dishes to choose from – try the pork miso katsu*, the grilled salmon in miso or the veggie and seafood tempura.

Beyond bento boxes, seafood is another speciality at Shyun. Chef Tom Suzuki heads a talented team that serves up market-fresh dishes that are, quite simply, works of art. The kingfish sashimi, sushi and sashimi platter, and Shyun hand rolls (featuring salmon *and* prawn) are all superb. Other must-try dishes include the soft-shell-crab sushi rolls or chicken karaage* for entrée, and the prawn tempura with udon noodles or the salmon don* for main.

The only drawback to Shyun is that it's neither licensed nor BYO, but with most dishes costing under $15, you'll have plenty of leftover dough for a cheeky nightcap afterwards.

> FEELING PECKISH?

126 Koornang Rd, Carnegie
(03) 9569 6530
www.shyun.net.au
Open Tues–Thurs 12–4pm & 5–9pm, Fri 12–4pm & 5–9.30pm, Sat 12–9.30pm, Sun 12–8.30pm

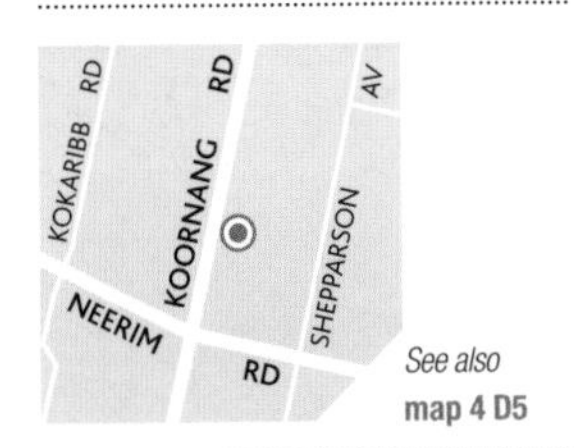

See also **map 4 D5**

'ENCYCLO' TRIVIA

* Bento boxes, or obento, are a popular Japanese lunchtime meal. The boxes are divided into compartments that are filled with rice, vegetables (cooked, pickled or raw), and fish or meat dishes.

* Miso is a sweet and salty type of Japanese seasoning, often used to make soup and sauces. In this instance, it is a thick sauce, and katsu is fried pork coated in panko (Japanese breadcrumbs).

* Chicken karaage is marinated, coated in flour and then lightly fried.

* Don is short for donburi, which means 'bowl of rice with food on top'.

THIS WAY
manabar

NIGHT OWL

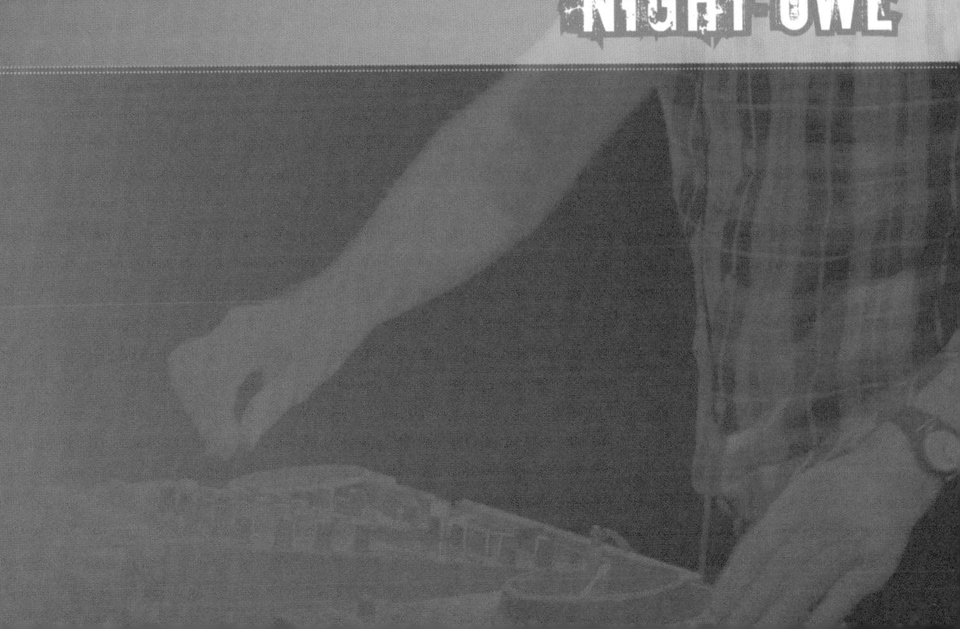

> NIGHT OWL

FINDING NETHERLAND

If the drunken theatrics, papier-mâché and boobies of the theatre-restaurant Dirty Dick's* fill your heart with glee (even if you've never heard of it, you know what I mean), then get down to the Bottom End at the bum end of Little Collins Street, quicksticks. The joint jumps with all the squares, beatniks, mods and teeny-boppers of a drive-in B-flick. Fake grottoes are adorned with bowers of fake plants and fake plaster Aphrodites (bosomy enough to elicit a grope and a 'phwoar!' from some irony-free King Street* lads at the bar).

An entertaining drinks list ranges from the tasty Americano (Campari, sweet vermouth and soda) to the intriguing Robert Mitchum (bourbon, maple syrup, orange juice and egg) and the bizarre Australian Martini (vodka, Cointreau, Vegemite, Coon cheese and pickled onion). If the siren song of trans fats proves irresistible after a few rounds of Clamato*, you may want to give the burger menu a once-over. Everything is cheese-filled and excellent value, and comes with a side of crinkle-cut chips to dip into tubs of bright-orange mayonnaise. A nice refresher after all this is a glass of wine described on the menu as either 'cheap', 'average' or 'good'.

The Bottom End is fairly new on the bar/pub/dive scene, and is waiting for the influx of dudes, students and boozehounds it was clearly designed for. Once a wool store, then a ravers' club and then an Irish pub, it will be interesting to see where the latest incarnation takes this unruly posterior of the CBD.

> NIGHT OWL

579 Little Collins St, Melbourne
(03) 9629 3001
thebottomend.com.au
Open Wed–Thurs 12pm–1am,
Fri 12pm–3am, Sat 6pm–5am

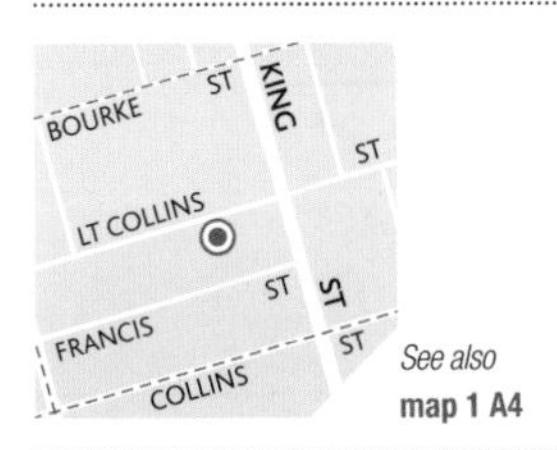

See also
map 1 A4

'ENCYCLO' TRIVIA

* Dirty Dick's is a medieval-style theatre-restaurant featuring saucy wenches and unrelenting double entendres.

* King Street is home to some seedy establishments in Melbourne's CBD. It's the place for girlie bars and, on unfortunate occasions, some violence between drunken louts.

* Clamato is a zesty mix of tomato juice, spices and clam broth.

> NIGHT OWL

CARAVAN MUSIC CLUB

A SOUNDTRACK FOR THE SOUTH

Hear that? That's the anguished howl of live-music fans south of the Yarra River, frustrated *yet again* at having to traipse north for their gig fix. True, there was a time (back when folks like Nick Cave and Paul Kelly were but whippersnappers) when St Kilda was a reliable source of south-side rock'n'roll action. But these days? Not so much.

Venture further south to downtown Oakleigh, however, and you'll discover an oasis in the musical desert: the Caravan Music Club. Conceived in response to the north side's monopoly on good gigs, this unique venue started life as the occasional show in manager Peter Foley's lounge room, before moving to the Oakleigh Bowling Club, and finally to its current home at the Oakleigh RSL*.

A live-music venue in an RSL? Sounds weird, but it works. Artists perform on a grand, arched stage in a fabulous Deco-styled hall, giving shows a sense of spectacle rarely found at your average pub or club gig. It's a treat for punters and musicians alike; no wonder readers of *Rhythms* magazine voted it Australia's top venue.

From American soul-screamer Barrence Whitfield to home-grown talents like Ed Kuepper and The Black Sorrows, it's all killer, not filler at the Caravan. They take their music seriously here, with a predilection for the good stuff – roots and soul, country and rock'n'roll – which means the dance floor is usually jumping. Tired? Catch your breath in the spacious beer garden while enjoying a refreshing, RSL-priced drink!

Suburbia may not be the new inner city just yet, but it's looking decidedly better since the Caravan Music Club moved in.

> NIGHT OWL

95–97 Drummond St, Oakleigh
0411 569 180
www.caravanmusic.com.au
Open according to scheduled gigs; see website for details

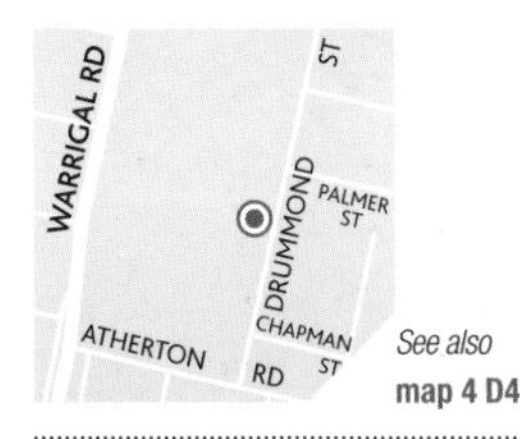

See also **map 4 D4**

'ENCYCLO' TRIVIA

* RSL stands for Returned and Services League of Australia. While originally set up for returned WW I servicemen, these days RSL clubs are places for social gatherings, bowls clubs and the like.

ENKIDU
DRANK SEVEN CUPS OF
BEER
AND HIS HEART
SOARED.
2600 B.C
The epic of Gilgamesh
WASHED
AND HUMAN
BECAME A

TEMPLE BREWERY & BRASSERIE

HOUSE OF FERVENT FERMENTATION

Come, people, come! All hail the benevolent spirit of the mighty hop, the frothy goodness of that most quenching beverage: beer.

It might be the world's oldest fermented beverage, but beer has been given a modern twist at Melbourne's newest place of worship: the Temple Brewery & Brasserie. Housed behind an obscure matt-black frontage with a carpark out front, it's not the most obvious place to come and pay homage. But once you're in the door and have the brewery's huge, state-of-the-art stainless steel vats in your sights, the beer penny drops.

Split over two levels, the bar is all dim lighting and polished-concrete floors. It's simple and modern and sleek, and leaves patrons free to focus on what this place is really all about: the beer. There are seven types on the go, which is a little overwhelming for an ingénue like me, so I opt for a bit of nearly everything with the $12 tasting wheel. It gives a 100 ml serve of five beers, and is an excellent accompaniment to the hearty goulash I've chosen from the small but classy food menu.

As I work my way through the beer wheel with a near-religious fervour, I conclude that the Bicycle Beer ('a light and refreshingly tart ale brewed with unmalted red wheat and flaked spelt') and Soba Ale ('a cold-fermented ale with the distinctive flavour of toasted buckwheat') are my kinds of brew. Amen.

> NIGHT OWL

122 Weston St, Brunswick East
(03) 9380 8999
www.templebrewing.com.au
Open Wed–Sat 11am–11pm, Sun 11am–9pm (hours vary, so double-check the website)

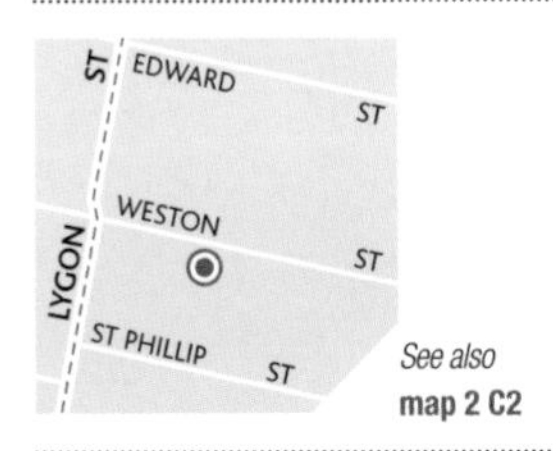

See also **map 2 C2**

COCO LOCO

Sometimes a glass of beer at your local just won't cut it. Sometimes it's a case of Piña Colada or bust. Wait, make that a Piña Colada served in a coconut shell – preferably somewhere exotic like a Polynesian beach. Which begs the question: what are we doing up the far end of Swan Street, a joyless strip of petrol stations and fast-food outlets? Believe it or not, this is the unlikely setting for Richmond's own slice of Polynesian paradise, Tiki Lounge and Bar.

Tucked away up a steep staircase, this cute 'n kitschy spot is one of the best-kept secrets in town. A magnificent bamboo bar takes pride of place, its shelves laden with top-quality liqueurs, spirits, mixers and tropical fruit. Magic happens here: time-honoured rum-based cocktails like the Mai Tai and the Zombie (so potent it comes with a two-per-person limit) are served in lurid tiki mugs, and perfect Piña Coladas come in – yep, you guessed it – coconut-shell cups. The refreshing Hemingway Daiquiri is tailor-made for literary types, while daring drinkers should try one of the sensational in-house creations (the flaming Ruapehu is inspired!). In true tiki tradition*, all cocktails are mixed to perfection and garnished to the hilt. Balancing indulgence with exertion, the bar also hosts regular tango and swing dance classes (check the website as these sometimes fall outside normal opening hours).

Bearing witness to your 'boozalicious' night out? A veritable pantheon of primitive island gods: fearsome tiki masks, enigmatic Easter Island moai* statuettes and other ancient idols occupy every available inch of wall and floor space. So get comfy on a couch (the nook near the aquarium is especially cosy) and raise your glass to them. Umgawa!*

> NIGHT OWL

327 Swan St, Richmond
(03) 9428 4336
tikiloungeandbar.com
Open Wed 6pm–12am, Fri–Sat 6pm–1am, Sun 6–10pm

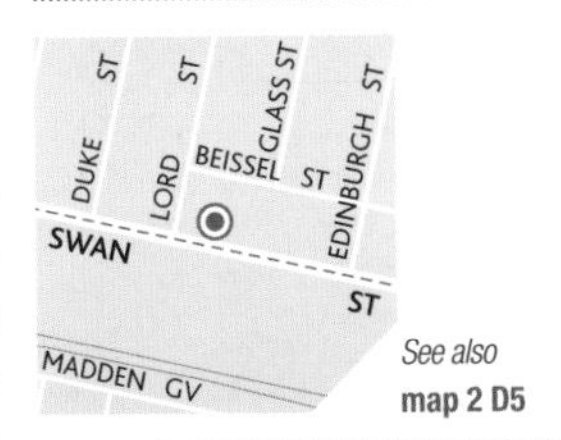

See also **map 2 D5**

'ENCYCLO' TRIVIA

* Tiki culture and Polynesian-themed bars were all the rage in mid-20th-century USA, with legendary figures like Don the Beachcomber and Trader Vic initiating an illustrious tradition of spectacular cocktails and bamboo exotica.

* Moai are otherwise known as those mysterious stone statues scattered around Easter Island.

* A term often used in a tiki-related context (as well as old Tarzan films), 'umgawa' can mean anything you want it to. Listen to 'Leilani' by the Hoodoo Gurus for inspiration …

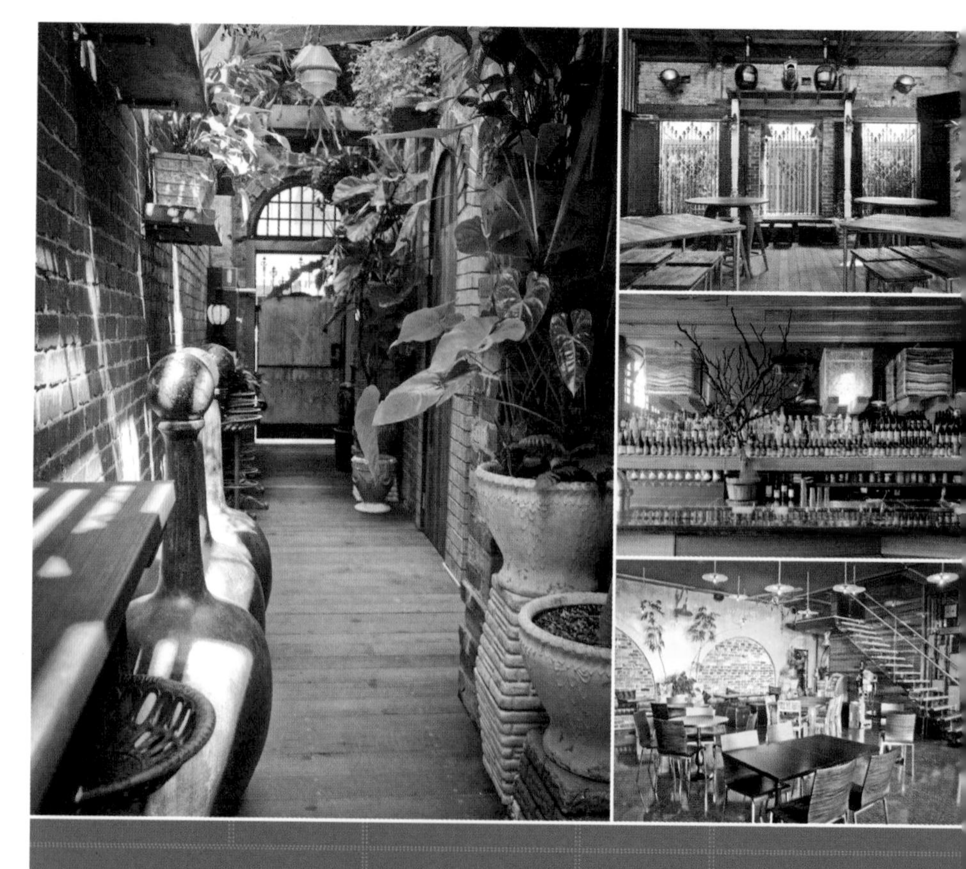

> NIGHT OWL

THE WOODLANDS HOTEL

NARNIA MEETS SYDNEY ROAD

There's a watering hole in the nether regions of Sydney Road giving its centrally located compadres a run for their pint-pulling, cork-popping money. All heritage building and old-man pub on the outside, inside it's a deliriously different story. For a start there's decor by local artist Blokk – he's the chap who helped give the Carlton Hotel in the city its Noah-sets-sail-in-a-bordello vibe*. The Woodlands Hotel is a tad more refined and tasteful, and it's also a little – OK, a lot – more wondrous.

Behold the bar, a rustic space hung with frilled, milk-glass light fittings and stocked with a 100% Victorian drinks list of the finest microbrews and wines our fair state has to offer. Be amazed by the light-filled back-room-slash-beer-garden, where a high, barn-like ceiling is broken up by skylights that can open right up to the actual sky. Be impressed by the upstairs restaurant, where you can indulge in the same menu on offer downstairs – with saliva-inducing dishes like gateaux piments*, ginger-infused kingfish, and potato-and-goat's-cheese dumplings – in distinctly regal surrounds. We're pleased to note that the prices remain the same in the upper echelons; it's just the service that goes up a notch (i.e. table service). Cue royal wave.

There's a platform above the beer garden, if you want to check the footy score on the TV or take a smoko break during your meal, along with winding staircases, secret doors, creeping vines and eyes in the walls. And there's art aplenty, and bathrooms you won't want to leave …

Intrigued? Impressed? Bamboozled? Excellent. It'll all make sense when you get here.

> NIGHT OWL

84–88 Sydney Rd, Coburg
(03) 9384 1122
www.thewoodlandshotel.com.au
Open Mon–Thurs 4pm–1am,
Fri–Sun 12pm–1am

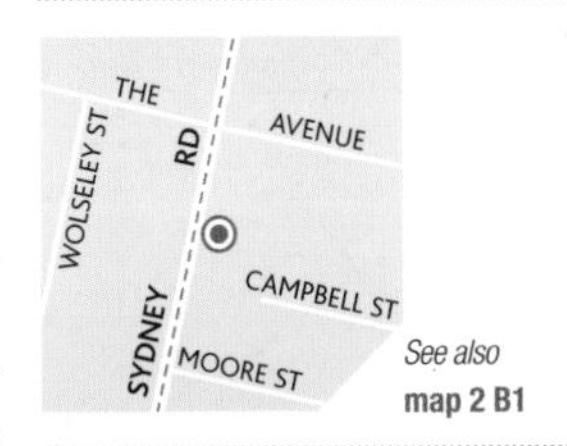

See also
map 2 B1

'ENCYCLO' TRIVIA

* The Carlton Hotel is a multilevel old dame at 193 Bourke St in the city that was transformed from dive to taxidermist's wet dream several years back.

* Gateaux piments is a Mauritian dish of spiced yellow-split-pea fritters with tomato salsa. It's a nod to the chef's country of origin.

LISTINO PREZZI
BAR AMERICANO
€
CAFFE 3 00
" 8 0 5 00
CAPPUCCINO 3 50
TEA 5 00
"
AMERICANO 16 00
POMPIER "
MAMMY TAYLOR "
BLOOD AND SAND 19 00
CLOVER CLUB "
HANKY PANKY "
CHICAGO FIZZ "
LAST WORD 21 00
OLD CUBAN "
VIEUX CARRE "
"
APERITIVO PROVIDED
"
AMARI 11 00
"
VINO 9 00
NO CREDIT CARD
NO SHOE NO SERVICE

> NIGHT OWL

BAR AMERICANO

STANDING ROOM ONLY, BELLA

You no speak Americano*? No worries – it's the language of liquor that counts at Bar Americano. And damn fine liquor it is too.

This tiny, Italian-all-the-way joint down a laneway fits a mere dozen or so people, so don't be getting fussy about settling in. In true Italian tradition, it's standing room only, designed for a good time, not a long one. It's open for drinks all day – coffee, that is, or perhaps a late-afternoon aperitif – but it's the night-time list of old-school cocktails like the Chicago Fizz (rum and port blended with lemon juice, sugar and egg whites), the Old Cuban (a minty, limey champagne-rum concoction) or the namesake Americano (Campari, sweet vermouth and soda) that'll have you lining up. The boozy drinks are served in glass jars and come steeped in history, many of them borrowed from books like *The Gentleman's Companion**. Which brings us to some sartorial suggestions: dress sharp, always wear shoes and go for style over stonewash.

Sure, this place might look like a cheap speakeasy from the laneway, but it's all class inside. Lean on the counter, if you must, and keep your camera-phone in your pocket: this is a place for discreet drinking, not happy snapping. And don't even think about paying with your credit card or trying to make a booking: this babe only accepts cold hard cash and isn't interested in a date. Mind you, there's always plenty of Hanky Panky* to be had.

> NIGHT OWL

20 Presgrave Pl, Melbourne
www.baramericano.com
Open Mon–Sat 8.30am–11pm

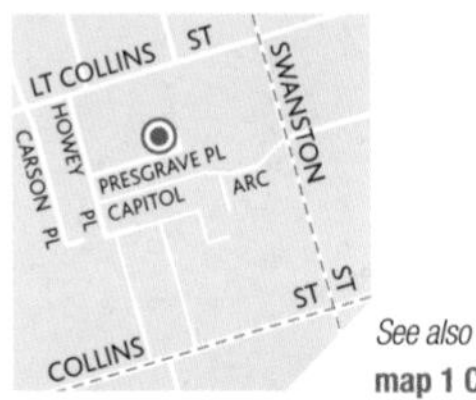

See also **map 1 C4**

'ENCYCLO' TRIVIA

* 'We No Speak Americano' was a hit in 2010 from the Australian band Yolanda Be Cool. It samples the 1956 Italian song 'Tu vuò fà l'Americano'.

* *The Gentleman's Companion* is a book written by food and drink aficionado Charles H. Baker, first published in 1939. His adventurous cocktail recipes have become the holy grail of many a cocktail list at sophisticated city bars.

* The Hanky Panky cocktail is a cheeky mix of gin, sweet vermouth and Fernet-Branca (a bitter, syrupy Italian liqueur).

LHMU
RTBU
ANF
Unions
Work

MR MCCLELLAND'S FINISHING SCHOOL

NOTHING FORMAL ABOUT THIS SHINDIG

I had my first pash at a school disco and without going into too much detail, it almost scarred me for life. But that didn't stop me hitting the wooden dance floor at Mr McClelland's Finishing School, a fortnightly Friday affair that is part school formal, part blue-light disco and part super-fun journey back into the music that was – if you're anything like me – the saving grace of your teenage years.

Held in the airy, high-ceilinged surrounds of the Bella Union's 19th-century ballroom, Finishing School packs in around 220 hot bods getting their high-school freak on. The music ranges from old-school and modern indie, to '60s rock and soul, to '90s grunge and eclectic pop tunes – think hit makers like The Smiths, Prince, Radiohead, Pulp, Sophie Ellis-Bextor and The Supremes.

Selector* Andrew McClelland day walks* as a comedian, and is a regular on TV shows like *Spicks and Specks* and *The Circle*. He started Finishing School in 2009, and keeps it real – '90s style – by playing tracks in their original form from CDs (you'll hear no mash-ups or electro vomit here). Tickets are just $10 at the door; get in early to avoid queues. Bella Union has a well-stocked bar, so leave the goon bag* at home.

Now, just for the record, I'm still OK with pashing – which is just as well, because at Finishing School just about anything goes. Take a look at Mr McClelland bouncing around the stage in a shirt and tie, ripping out dance moves inspired by some daggy old science teacher. I don't know which finishing school* *he* attended, but I sure as hell like it.

> NIGHT OWL

Bella Union, Level 1, Trades Hall, cnr Victoria & Lygon sts, Carlton South
(03) 9650 5699
www.bellaunion.com.au
Open every second Fri 9.30pm–1am

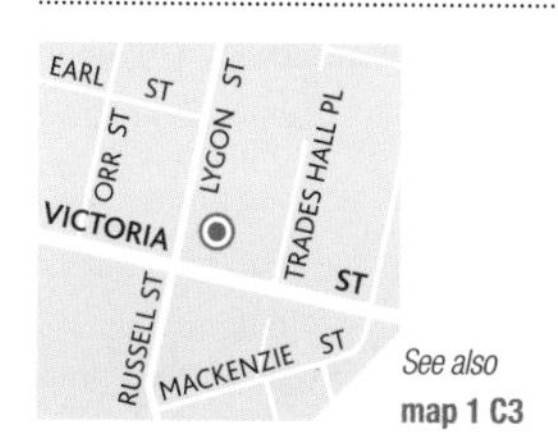

See also **map 1 C3**

'ENCYCLO' TRIVIA

* A selector is someone who selects and plays tracks, as opposed to a DJ who mixes and mashes them up.

* A day walker is a vampire who's able to walk in sunlight without being burned. In this case, we mean it's Mr McClelland's day job.

* A goon bag is that floppy silver bladder with a tap that you find inside a cask-wine box. It's super classy (not).

* An old-fashioned concept, finishing school is where well-bred ladies go after completing ordinary school to learn all about social and cultural etiquette.

MONOPOLY
YAHTZEE
SCRABBLE ORIGINAL
BATTLESHIP
JS

THE RACCOON CLUB

LOCAL AND LOVIN' IT

Preston's location – straddling Bell Street, that dividing line between cool inner city and outer suburbia – means it's a little starved for attention, poor thing. While all the limelight is hogged by nearby suburbs like Northcote and Brunswick, bursting with hip bars and restaurants, all Preston really wanted was a good watering hole to call its own. And with the opening of the Raccoon Club, that's exactly what it got.

The secrets to the Raccoon Club's success – aside from the owners' nous to plug that market gap – are a charming atmosphere, a killer beverage list and the creation of a true local*. The long industrial workshop space has been converted into a cosy retreat complete with comfy lounges, pool table, a crackling fireplace and a cracking turntable. Locals can punch themselves in and out on the workshop's old manual timekeeping clock, but there's no reward program here – this place is its own reward. And judging by the fact that the bar is decorated with raccoon-themed artworks donated by Preston punters, the locals find it very rewarding indeed.

As befits such a locally oriented bar, the drinks list has a strong focus on the regional and handmade, with craft beers from down the road (Thornbury's 3 Ravens) and a little further afield (West Heidelberg's Kooinda Pale Ale), and exclusive ciders from Seven Oaks in Merricks North. The wine list is 100% Victorian, and the harder stuff* is also Australian wherever possible. And get this: you can have meals delivered to the Club from the local Indian and pizza joints. When they talk about keeping it local here, they really mean it.

> NIGHT OWL

145 Plenty Rd, Preston
0433 827 003
Open Tues–Wed 5–11pm, Thurs–Fri 5pm–1am, Sat 2pm–1am, Sun 2–11pm

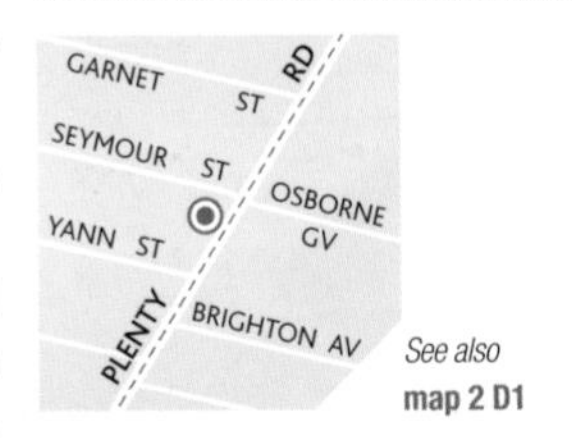

See also **map 2 D1**

'ENCYCLO' TRIVIA

* Don't be put off by the fact that this bar is a true local: non-Prestonites are also welcomed with open arms.

* Did you know that Australia has a burgeoning craft spirits industry?

> NIGHT OWL

IT'S ALL IN YOUR HEAD

Pardon me? You said you've been here since last week? No? You didn't realise I was such a geek? Yeah, well … Oh? Do I know how to gleek*? Whaa? I'm sorry, it's really loud in here … I said, IT'S REALLY LOUD IN HERE! … *Ooooh!* You read about this in *Hide & Seek!*

Yes, you did, party lover. And since you made like a banana split and took your fruity self to the Silent Disco, hasn't your world become a better place? Because at Silent Disco, you can choose from one of three live sets being spun by some of Australia's best DJs. You can adjust the volume yourself. You can dance to the same tunes as your friends, or find your own groove. You can have a conversation at normal pitch, and you can dance like there's no tomorrow. And it's all thanks to a genius idea – headphones.

This brilliant concept was brought home to Melbourne from Europe by a guy called Paul with the enviable job title 'Director of Fun'. When you arrive at the disco, you're fitted with a set of wireless headphones, given a quick lesson, then let loose on the dance floor. It happens at various hot spots around Melbourne – sometimes in pubs and bars, and sometimes in less likely locations like parks, rooftops, the beach, your backyard. Because that's the beauty of Silent Disco: it's, um, silent. But don't be fooled: the music might only happen in your head, but the party will be rocking all around you.

> NIGHT OWL

Various locations around Melbourne
1300 734 726 (that's 1300 7 DISCO, folks)
www.silentdiscomelbourne.com
See website for upcoming events

'ENCYCLO' TRIVIA

* To gleek is to spit using the salivary glands under the tongue; also slang for a fan of the TV show *Glee*.

> **NIGHT OWL**

DON'T KNOW MANA? YOU MUST BE A NOOB*

Gaming (or playing computer games) is generally considered one of the most antisocial pastimes you can get caught up in. Awake until all hours, bathed in the glow of a monitor, surrounded by empty fast-food containers and cans of Red Bull, clutching a well-worn controller and yelling threats into a headset is how most people picture your typical gamer …

But it doesn't have to be like this! And Mana Bar is the proof. Reminiscent in equal parts of a speakeasy, electronic store's TV department and your best mate's share-house lounge room, Mana is a fairly unassuming little bar by day. Come night-time though, it's abuzz with groups of friends locking heads over video games across a multitude of platforms (like PlayStation 3, Xbox 360 and Nintendo Wii). The crowd of curious onlookers who gather outside the glowing front window will attest to that!

Strategically placed screens and consoles line Mana's blue walls alongside an impressively stocked bar. Games on offer are the latest and greatest and are changed around each month; there's also some old-school stuff for those so inclined. Special events are held for big-game releases and the bi-weekly trivia night attracts some of the most unpretentious barflies you're ever likely to meet.

But it's the extra little details that make Mana Bar worth a visit. Take the creative cocktail and shot lists, for instance, where drinks have names like Finish Him (a Bloody Mary–type concoction bound to be popular with Mortal Kombat players). And the bathrooms are worth a squiz too, with geek-specific vandalism and gamer in-jokes demonstrating that Mana's definitely resonating with its target demographic – and taking the anti out of antisocial in the process.

> NIGHT OWL

336 Brunswick St, Fitzroy
(03) 9417 3432
www.manabar.com.au
Open Tues–Sun 3–11pm

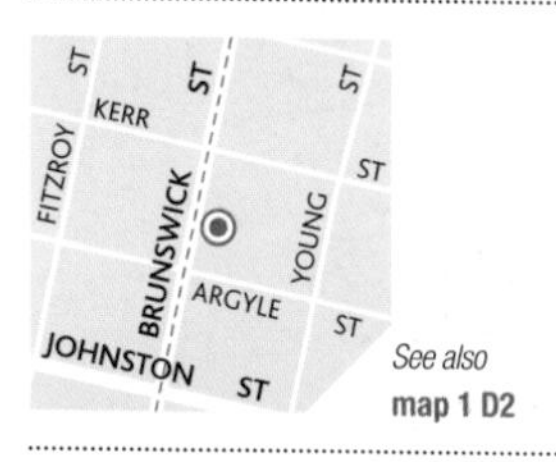

See also **map 1 D2**

'ENCYCLO' TRIVIA

* Noob is short for newbie, a rookie or novice in gaming who is generally regarded as not worthy of established players' time.

YOUR OWN MELBOURNE DISCOVERIES

PHOTOGRAPHY CREDITS

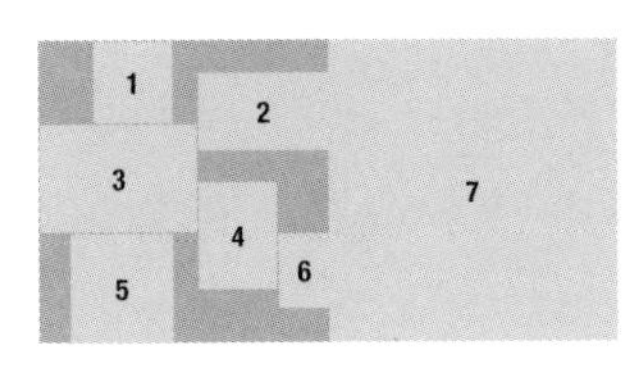

HIT THE STREETS

1, 3 & 5 Erika Budiman
2 Lachie Challis
4 Victoria Fox
6 Jonathan White
7 Courtesy of the Sun Theatre

TRAM SESSIONS

Photos by Erika Budiman

MISS FOX

Photos by Victoria Fox

THE SUBSTATION

Photos by Erika Budiman

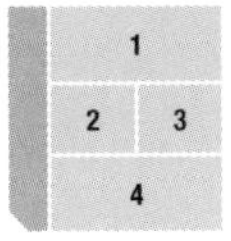

SOLAR SYSTEM WALK

1 & 4 Erika Budiman
2–3 Courtesy of City of Port Phillip

MAILBOX 141

Photos by Erika Budiman

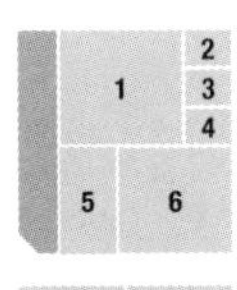

SUN THEATRE

1–2 & 4–6 Courtesy of the Sun Theatre
3 Erika Budiman

FROCKS ON BIKES

Photos by Jonathan White

VINYASA PLAYLIST

Photos by Lachie Challis

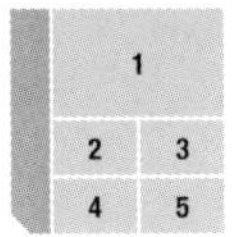

FOOTSCRAY COMMUNITY ARTS CENTRE

1–2 & 4–5 Courtesy of Footscray Community Arts Centre
3 Rachel Main

RICKETTS POINT MARINE SANCTUARY

Photo by Samantha Wilson

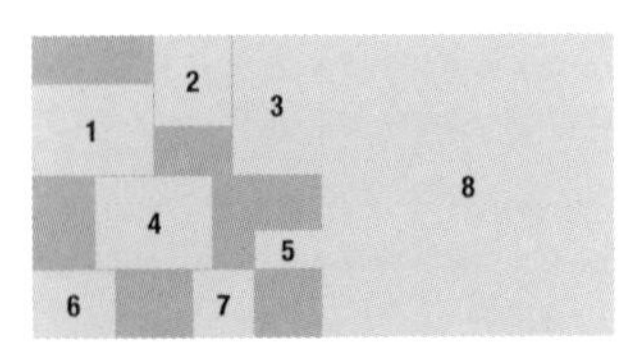

TREASURE TROVE

1 Courtesy of Signed & Numbered
2–7 Erika Budiman
8 Kristyna Hessova

DEJOUR JEANS

Photos by Erika Budiman

WOOLY BULLY

Photos by Erika Budiman

SO:ME SPACE

Photos by Kristyna Hessova

THE GOOD BREW COMPANY

Photo courtesy of the Good Brew Company

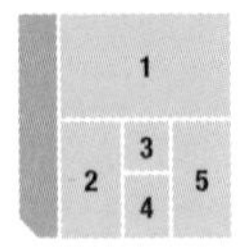

MAGIC LANTERN STUDIO

1 Louise M. Cooper
2–5 Erika Budiman

FROCKS AND SLACKS

Photos by Erika Budiman

VILLAGE IDIOM

Photos by Erika Budiman

PATCHWORK ON CENTRAL PARK

Photos by Erika Budiman

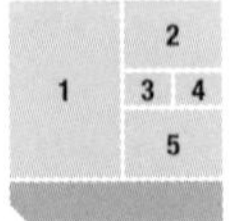

SIGNED & NUMBERED

1 & 3–5 Erika Budiman
2 Courtesy of Signed & Numbered

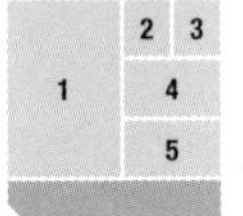

SHELLEY PANTON

1–3 Christina Mitchell
4–5 Laura Manariti

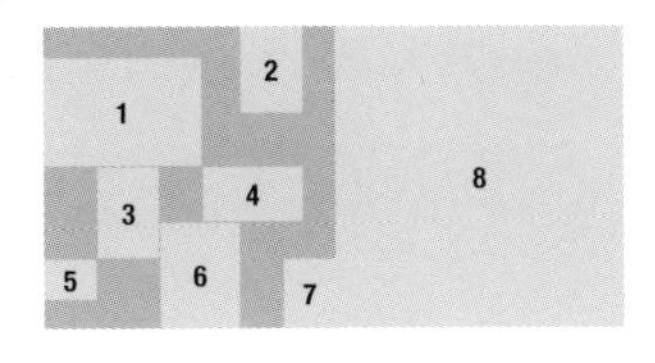

FEELING PECKISH?

1–5 & 7–8 Erika Budiman
6 Victoria Simson

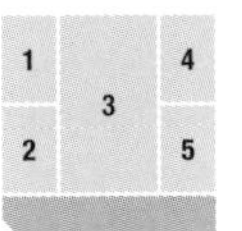

ELCEED

1–2 & 4–5 Erika Budiman
3 Hannah Collinson

GUMBO KITCHEN

Photos by Erika Budiman

MIDDLE FISH

Photos by Erika Budiman

AL ALBERO

Photos by Erika Budiman

FONDA MEXICAN

Photos by Victoria Simson

DARAC BAR & GRILL

Photos by Erika Budiman

BACKSTREET CAFE

Photos by Erika Budiman

FAMOUS BLUE RAINCOAT

Photos by Erika Budiman

MICHELANGELO

Photos by Erika Budiman

SHYUN

Photos by Erika Budiman

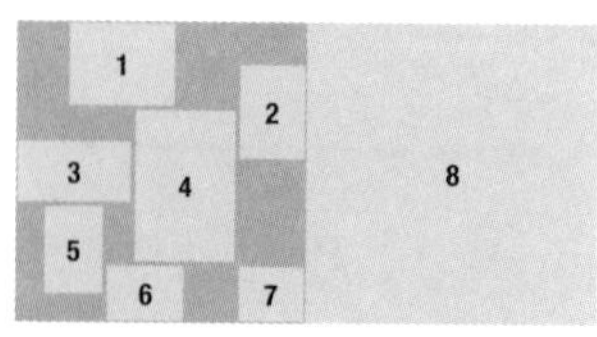

NIGHT OWL

1 Courtesy of Mana Bar
2 Courtesy of the Bottom End
3–8 Erika Budiman

THE BOTTOM END

1 & 3 Scott Newett
2 & 4 Courtesy of the Bottom End

CARAVAN MUSIC CLUB

Photos by Erika Budiman

TEMPLE BREWERY & BRASSERIE

Photos by Teagan Glenane

TIKI LOUNGE AND BAR

Photos by Erika Budiman

THE WOODLANDS HOTEL

Photos by Amy Braybrook

BAR AMERICANO

Photos by Michael Brady

MR MCCLELLAND'S FINISHING SCHOOL

Photos by Erika Budiman

THE RACCOON CLUB

Photos by Erika Budiman

SILENT DISCO

Photos by Anne di Paolo

MANA BAR

Photos courtesy of Mana Bar

OTHER BOOKS IN THE SERIES

Available at all good bookstores, newsagents, giftshops and online at **www.hideseek.com.au**

ACKNOWLEDGEMENTS

The publisher would like to acknowledge the following individuals and organisations:

Publications manager: Astrid Browne

Managing editor: Melissa Krafchek

Design and photo selection: Erika Budiman

Editor: Michelle Bennett

Writers: Vanessa Murray, Samantha Wilson, Chad Parkhill, Dale Campisi, Jana Raus, Ryan Smith, Michael Brady, Rebecca L. Stewart

Cartography: Emily Maffei, Bruce McGurty

Layout: Megan Ellis

Pre-press: Megan Ellis, PageSet Digital Print & Pre-press

PHOTOGRAPHY CREDITS

Cover (clockwise from main image): Middle Fish, Carlton (Erika Budiman); Cocktail at Tiki Lounge and Bar, Richmond (Erika Budiman); Records at Wooly Bully, North Melbourne (Erika Budiman); Barbecued corn at Fonda Mexican, Richmond (Victoria Simson); Exterior of the Substation, Newport (Erika Budiman)

Back cover: Loving life at a Footscray Community Arts Centre event, Footscray (Courtesy of Footscray Community Arts Centre)

Half-title page: Jam jar filled with horchata and ice at Fonda Mexican, Richmond (Victoria Simson)

Title pages: The Woodlands Hotel, Coburg (Amy Braybrook)

About this guide: Mailbox 141, Nicholas Building, Melbourne (Erika Budiman)

Explore Australia Publishing Pty Ltd
Ground Floor, Building 1, 658 Church Street, Richmond, VIC 3121

Explore Australia Publishing Pty Ltd is a division of Hardie Grant Publishing Pty Ltd

Published by Explore Australia Publishing Pty Ltd, 2012

A Cataloguing-in-Publication entry is available from the catalogue of the National Library of Australia at www.nla.gov.au

DISCLAIMER

While every care is taken to ensure the accuracy of the data within this product, the owners of the data (including the state, territory and Commonwealth governments of Australia) do not make any representations or warranties about its accuracy, reliability, completeness or suitability for any particular purpose and, to the extent permitted by law, the owners of the data disclaim all responsibility and all liability (including without limitation, liability in negligence) for all expenses, losses, damages, (including indirect or consequential damages) and costs which might be incurred as a result of the data being inaccurate or incomplete in any way and for any reason.

ISBN-13 9781741174007

10 9 8 7 6 5 4 3 2 1

Printed and bound in China by 1010 Printing International Ltd

Publisher's note: Every effort has been made to ensure that the information in this book is accurate at the time of going to press. The publisher welcomes information and suggestions for correction or improvement. Email: info@hideseek.com.au

Publisher's disclaimer: The publisher cannot accept responsibility for any errors or omissions. The representation on the maps of any road or track is not necessarily evidence of public right of way. The publisher cannot be held responsible for any injury, loss or damage incurred during travel. It is vital to research any proposed trip thoroughly and seek the advice of relevant state and travel organisations before you leave.

www.hideseek.com.au
Follow us on Twitter: @HideandSeekAU
Find us on Facebook: www.facebook.com/HideSeekau